A Year of Walks: Cheshire

Clive Price

Published by Sigma Leisure – an imprint of
Sigma Press, 1 South Oak Lane, Wilmslow, Cheshire SK9 6AR, England.

British Library Cataloguing in Publication Data
A CIP record for this book is available from the British Library.

ISBN: 1-85058-710-8

Typesetting and Design by: Sigma Press, Wilmslow, Cheshire.

Cover photographs: clockwise, from top left – the village green, Astbury; Clarence Mill, Bollington; Shutlingsloe, near Wildboarclough; a winter scene near Kettleshulme *(all photographs by Graham Beech)*
Cover design: MFP Design and Print
Photographs within the book: Clive Price
Maps: Michael Gilbert

Printed by: MFP Design and Print

Acknowledgments

No author is an island unto himself and this is certainly true in my case. This volume would never have been completed without the unstinting assistance and forbearance of others who, in their various ways, have contributed to its publication. Every one of them has made their particular expertise freely available to me.

Firstly I must acknowledge my gratitude to Graham Beech and the staff of Sigma Press for their encouragement and professional skills from the moment when this book was little more than a germ of an idea to the day when the finished product appeared. I am also most grateful for their understanding during a personal crisis which delayed the production of the manuscript.

Thanks are also due to Dr Andre Farrar of the RSPB's North-West office for his willing supply of information about the birds of the Dee Estuary and Gayton Sands in particular and throughout the county in general. Other people who have answered numerous queries have been the staffs of the public libraries in Manchester, Chester, Wilmslow and Macclesfield as well as those of the Tourist Information Centres scattered throughout Cheshire.

Some of these particular routes may not have been included were it not for the rapid response of Dave Kitching, Chief Countryside Officer for Cheshire County Council, and his staff. Whenever I reported a footpath problem it was dealt with expeditiously and the right of passage opened-up. Chris Bamsey, Countryside Ranger based at Teggs Nose, supplied invaluable information on Macclesfield Forest.

Finally, but by no means least, my gratitude must be expressed to various members of my family who have accompanied me on some of the walks. In particular, my granddaughter Tamsin, who, as usual, has made many useful observations which otherwise would have been missed and which have subsequently been incorporated into the text. Their companionship has been keenly appreciated.

Clice Price

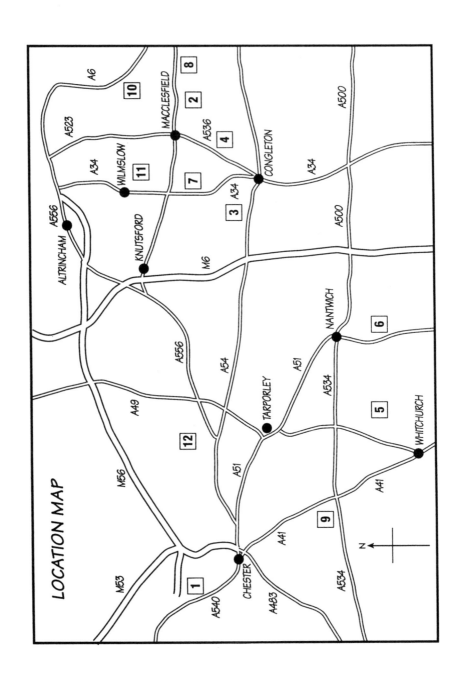

LOCATION MAP

Contents

The Walks

The Wirral
Distance: 12½ miles (20 kilometres)

Macclesfield Forest
Distance: 5½ miles (8.8 kilometres)

Swettenham
Distance: 8 miles (12½ kilometres) or 5 miles (8 kilometres)

Gawsworth
Distance: 7½ miles (12 kilometres)

Marbury
Distance: 5 miles (8 kilometres)

Audlem
Distance: 5 miles (8 kilometres)

Introduction

Walking is not a seasonal activity: it is enjoyable on every day of the year, no matter what the weather. The occasional walker who ventures out on a fine Spring day will feel exhilarated by the first flush of greenery on the hedgerow or, on a sunny Autumn day, will marvel at the richness and variety of the colours, but the regular year-round walker will observe the subtler changes wrought by the gradually rising or falling temperatures and the lengthening or shortening of the daylight hours.

The starkness of the winter scene in the countryside is as wonderful as the lushness of high summer but it does not arrive suddenly. It evolves, almost on a daily basis. These changes in the appearance of the landscape also affect the flora and the fauna. The first signs of the mating ritual of the birds are evident to the keen observer in January, sometimes even in December. The song of the robin alters with the approach of the breeding season and the herons commence their nest building long before the first egg is laid.

New summer visitors arrive on a daily, almost hourly, basis during the Spring and depart as gradually as the days shorten. From September onwards other species arrive to take their place so that the ornithological interest of Winter is sharply different from that of Summer and, in some ways and in some places, far more abundant. Other birds appear but for a short while as they pass through the country to other wintering sites and only the regular walker will be in a position to notice them.

The first intimations of new growth appear during the long dark days of Winter when shoots break through the soil and then snowdrops and crocus burst into flower. The butterbur flowers in February, long before it acquires those rhubarb-like leaves. Frogs and other amphibians begin to migrate to their breeding sites while the trees are still leafless and badgers start to venture forth from their winter quarters. Other mammals are active all year round.

In the countryside there are no firm and fast rules: annual fluctuations in the weather guarantee that no two years are alike. Severe frosts and heavy snowfalls have no guaranteed dates and may delay

the appearance of certain flowers: strong winds and gales may delay
the arrival of migrant birds. The appearance of the landscape is altered by the weather. It is obviously different when covered with a
carpet of snow than when it is parched and scorched after a long and
severe drought. A clear blue sky with bright sunshine will enhance
the aspect whereas a cloak of gun-metal grey cloud will shroud
fields and moors with a drabness to match.

England is noted for its fickle weather so that sudden changes
may alter views within minutes. Such alterations are the prerogative
of the year-round walker who ventures forth in all weathers to appreciate the subtleties of the rural scene. It is for this reason that references are made to weather lore, because many of the ancient saws
were framed by our rural forbears who were so dependent on the
weather for the success or failure of their crops. Their meteorological observations were based on long practical experience and an in-
timate relationship with their particular area and environment.

The individual routes in this collection of walks have been chosen to highlight the changing moods and patterns of the landscape
throughout the year. They also aim to reveal some of the beauty and
charms of rural Cheshire throughout the seasons.

Cheshire

Scenically Cheshire is a county of startling contrasts. Initially the
name conjures up images of lush green pastures grazed by Friesian
cattle and dotted with black and white timber-framed houses. In re-
ality, it offers a variety few other counties can parallel from the
rough, rugged gritstone uplands in the east to the wild, haunting
coastline of the Dee estuary in the west. The central plain, noted for
its clays and marls, is broken by such sandstone upthrusts as Alderley Edge, Bickerton Hill, Helsby Hill and the Peckforton Hills. One of
its greatest attractions is Delamere Forest.

The county is blessed with an abundance of water. There are several meandering rivers including the Dee, the Mersey, the Bollin, the
Dane, the Gowy and the Weaver. The Industrial Revolution of the
eighteenth Century saw the construction of a network of important
canals: the Bridgewater, the Trent and Mersey, the Macclesfield and
the Shropshire Union. The tow paths of these, all repaired and up-

graded in recent years by British Waterways, provide miles of routes for the walker. Today, commercial traffic has been replaced by the pleasure boats.

The many meres, some large and some small, which have been created by land subsidence and ice-melt over millions of years, have all attracted numerous forms of avian and riparian wildlife to provide yet another dimension of interest for the wanderer through Cheshire's countryside.

This rural landscape is dotted with fascinating buildings ranging from stately homes to humble cottages, from inspiring churches to impressive mills, some of which have been transformed into working museums. Styal Mill, Little Alderley Mill, Stretton Mill, Little Moreton Hall, Lyme Hall, Tatton Hall and Dunham Massey are but a selection of these ubiquitous attractions.

Since Roman times, perhaps even earlier, the county has been noted for the production of salt, an industry which has given its name to such towns as Northwich, Nantwich and Middlewich. For its transport, a network of saltways was created, packhorse routes which still enable the rambler to explore some remote and beautiful corners of the countryside that the car cannot reach.

Cheshire's other famous product is cheese using the rich milk produced by all those Friesian cows grazing the fertile meadows of the central plain. Specialist manufacturers still produce it according to traditional recipes and, for the hungry walker, it is invariably on the menu at the cafes and inns suggested for each walk.

In more recent times, Cheshire has developed an industrial belt along its northern fringe stretching from Altrincham through Northwich and Widnes to Ellesmere Port. The basis of this is chemicals but the building of the Manchester Ship Canal accentuated this growth and, around Stanlow, Cheshire boasts one of the largest oil refinery complexes in the country, if not in the world.

Although there are odd pockets of industry elsewhere, such as Nantwich and Crewe with its Rolls Royce and the railway works, the area to the south of the A556, the old Manchester to Chester road, is the most rural and the most attractive. It is for that reason that most, though not all, of the walks included in this selection are to be found south of that line.

The Walks

These walks have been selected with a view to enhancing the joys and pleasures to be derived from walking through Cheshire in every month of the year. For anyone in search of a real challenge, some of the routes traverse the rough, windswept upland moors in the east of the county, often within the boundaries of the Peak District National Park. Others, lacking in long or steep uphill stretches, compensate by their very length. Some are so short that they may be considered little more than an afternoon or evening stroll, ideal for the younger members of the family. Whilst by no means exhaustive of the county's extensive network of footpaths, they cover all the major aspects of the countryside and scenery which Cheshire has to offer.

They all follow Public Rights of Way as depicted on Ordnance Survey maps, occasionally using sections of designated trails such as the Gritstone or the Sandstone or disused railway tracks which have been converted into walking routes. Some of the routes make use of concessionary paths opened up by the relevant landowner, often under the Countryside Agency's Countryside Stewardship scheme.

Where appropriate, especially as links where no other paths exist, canal tow paths have been utilised. Although stretches of road have had to be used to connect certain paths, I have tried to avoid their use because of the inherent dangers posed by traffic.

Tourist Information

Like any other county Cheshire boasts a wide array of tourist attractions from the sites owned by English Heritage and the National Trust to others which are in private ownership. They include prehistoric sites, Roman remains, medieval castles and abbeys and stately homes. There are different attractions such as working farms, candle workshops, country parks, industrial and local museums, garden centres and craft workshops. One or two are most unusual. Amongst these are the Anderton Boat Lift, Jodrell Bank and an arboretum. Many have been established or opened-up as part of the burgeoning tourist industry.

Details of some of these, where relevant, have been included in the text but further information about all of them may be obtained from any of the Tourist Information Centres listed below.

ⓘ **Chester TIC,** Town Hall, Northgate Street, Chester CH1 2QP. Phone: 01244 603107

ⓘ **Congleton TIC,** Town Hall, High Street, Congleton CW12 1BN. Phone: 01260 271095.

ⓘ **Ellesmere Port TIC,** Council Offices, Civic Way, Ellesmere Port L65 0BE. Phone: 0151 355 3665.

ⓘ **Knutsford TIC,** Council Offices, Toft Road, Knutsford WA16 6TA. Phone: 01565 632611.

ⓘ **Vale Royal TIC,** Wyvern House, The Drumber, Winsford CW7 1AH. Phone: 01606 862862.

ⓘ **Nantwich TIC,** Church House, The Square, Nantwich, Phone: 01270 610983.

ⓘ **Macclesfield TIC,** Town Hall, Macclesfield, SK10 1DX. Phone: 01625 504114/ 504115.

Many libraries also have tourist information points which stock leaflets and brochures with details of local attractions.

Public Transport

Many, although not all, of these routes are accessible by public transport. Relevant details concerning bus or train services are provided at the appropriate points in the text. However, since the de-regulation of bus services and the privatisation of the railways, many of these services are subject to frequent changes, especially with the introduction of new government initiatives concerning rural transport.

Cheshire County Council publishes a series of bus and train timetables covering the entire county but even these may become out-of-date very quickly. These are obtainable at Tourist Information Centres or from the Tourism and Marketing Unit at Commerce House, Hunter Street, Chester.

For the most accurate and up-to-date information contact one of the Cheshire Bus Hotlines:

ⓘ **Wilmslow:** 01625 534850.

ⓘ **Crewe:** 01270 505350

ⓘ **Chester:** 01244 602666

ⓘ **Northwich:** 01606 815050.

Detailed information about train times and routes may be obtained from Rail Enquiries: 0345 484950.

Clothing and Equipment

These walks are designed to be undertaken at all times of the year. Therefore, appropriate seasonal clothing will be necessary. This will improve your comfort considerably and so, your enjoyment. Obviously, to a certain extent, the choice of clothing is a matter of personal taste but there are some general guidelines. Jeans, for example, are not advisable in wet cold weather because, if they become saturated with water, they may become a serious hazard in fighting hypothermia.

Even in lowland Cheshire good footwear is essential and should take the form of either walking boots or shoes with a good, firm grip. This is particularly the case where paths are wet and muddy, especially after a prolonged period of wet weather. Boots will provide better ankle support on rough, stony ground. Any good stockist will offer advice and a wide range to choose from at varying prices.

Not only are the walks designed for the year-round outdoor enthusiast. but the English climate is noted for being extremely fickle. It can be as warm in January as in July and snow is not unknown in Cheshire even as late as June. From this it follows that a shell jacket or cagoule and over-trousers should be carried at all times. Once again it is advisable to go for quality when buying and today there is a wide selection of outer garments made from breathable, waterproof fabrics such as Gore-Tex™.

An extra pullover is another essential because the temperature is always a few degrees lower on the hill tops than on the plain or in the valley. This selection of walks ranges from sea level to altitudes in excess of 1,500 feet.

Always carry a first-aid kit to treat minor cuts and bruises. These may occur anywhere, especially in negotiating stiles with barbed wire adjacent. Another useful tool is a small pocket knife. In case of emergency when it is necessary to summon help, a whistle is extremely useful.

Although you may plan to have a meal after the walk is completed, always carry some emergency rations in the form of chocolate bars to provide extra nourishment and energy in case of unexpected delays. They are also enjoyable during a coffee break. A good day sack should prove more than ample for carrying all the equipment needed on these particular walks.

Maps

All the walks in this collection are based on Public Rights of Way as shown on the Ordnance Survey Outdoor Leisure and Pathfinder series of maps. However, at the time of writing the Pathfinder maps are being replaced gradually by the newer Explorer series. These are of the same 1:25 000 scale but each sheet covers a much larger area, so making them more economical. Almost all of Cheshire is now covered by the new mapping and the appropriate Explorer references are given.

Extra Information

In addition to the route directions each chapter includes information about places of interest along the way in the belief that such material adds considerably to the enjoyment of a day out in the open air. Walking is not simply a case of striding out but of enjoying the surroundings and absorbing the interest to be encountered. Most people are fascinated by strange buildings, stately homes, mills and similar attractions. The notes are not intended to be exhaustive but, for those seeking to develop their interest further, the local library will probably have a selection of books on the particular topic and the staff will be willing to advise.

In the same vein the notes on each particular month of the year have been included in the hope that they will add to the walker's enjoyment. In references to the weather and the wildlife I have tried to take the norm but, as these two factors are intertwined and react on each other, there are always exceptions. Flowers, for instance, rarely burst into bloom on the same date each year and it is one of the intriguing aspects of the countryside that we notice that certain natural events often appear to be either earlier or later than usual.

Where applicable I have included information on folklore and legend because these, too, in their own way, add to the rich weave of fabric that makes rural England a place of absorbing and never-ending interest.

Finally, whether you undertake each walk during the suggested month or not, enjoy your outing in this charming corner of England. You will probably see things that eluded me.

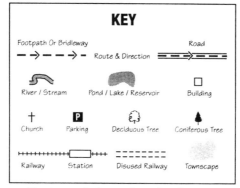

Key to symbols used on sketch maps

January

The Wirral

This low-level walk follows a disused railway track and shoreline paths affording excellent views of the Dee Estuary and the thousands of wildfowl which spend their winters on the mudflats. For anyone not wishing to complete the whole circuit a return by bus is possible from several points.

Route: Willaston – Wirral Way – Cuckoo Lane – Little Neston – Old Quay – Neston – Parkgate – Gayton – Backwood Hall – Boathouse Lane – Brook House – Station Road – Lees Lane – Willaston.

Terrain: Disused railway track, field paths, bridleways, promenade and coastal paths. May be extremely muddy, especially after wet weather. No serious climbing.

Start: The Wirral Way car park, Hadlow Road, Willaston. Map reference 331773.

Distance: 12½ miles (20 kilometres)

Map: OS Explorer 266 - Wirral & Chester

Public Transport: Willaston, Little Neston and Parkgate are served by frequent daily buses from Meols, Chester and Ellesmere Port. No Sunday service.

By Car: The starting and finishing point is the car park in Hadlow Road, Willaston. This is signed from the A540 Chester to Hoylake road and from Willaston village centre as the Wirral Country Park. Willaston village is also signed from the A540, and lies on the B5133 between Neston and Hooton.

Refreshments: Aston's Tea Rooms in Willaston village are open daily all year. Monday to Saturday, 9.30 am to 5.30 pm and Sundays 11 am to 4 pm. There are several cafes in Parkgate and Neston and pubs in Willaston, Neston and Parkgate also serve meals.

The Month

The name January has evolved through Middle English and French from the Latin word Januarius meaning the month of Janus, Janus being the Roman god who guarded doors and entrances. The word

Janitor is derived from the same sources. Hence it is most appropriate for the first month of the year.

Following hard on the festivities of Christmas and the New Year, the remainder of January appears to be a long featureless month. Initially there is little perceptible lengthening of the days, many of which have little to offer except dull, grey skies. On average, it is the coldest month of the year and one in which there is likely to be snow and hard frosts. However, there are exceptions, and although many days produce little light, there may be prolonged periods of relative mildness and brilliant sunshine.

Unless blanketed by snow, the landscape appears dank and lifeless, littered with the still-decaying detritus of the previous year's growth. The oaks may have the occasional, shrivelled-up brown leaf still clinging to their otherwise bare branches but otherwise it is, like most other deciduous trees, little more than skeletal. Yet even these, seen against the bleak winter sunshine, present a haunting beauty unknown at no other time of year. The ground may be extremely muddy except during severe frosts when it becomes rough, hard and pitted.

As the days begin to lengthen slightly, there are signs that nature is not fully dormant. The holly and the ivy retain their green leaves and, by the close of the month there may be the initial flecks of green as the tiny buds of the hawthorn hedges commence their incipient emergence. It is not unusual to see the green shoots of daffodils thrusting up through the soil and snowdrops and even crocus may even be seen in flower, depending upon the temperatures.

While flocks of long-tailed tits, fieldfares and redwings may be more evident, the bullfinch visits the garden and there are subtle changes in the song of the robin as the first mating urges of the year begin to stir. Indeed, it is not unknown for starlings to have young this month and in Cheshire even blackbirds have been observed sitting eggs in their nests.

Despite appearances, much of nature never sleeps. A walk along a muddy lane or track will reveal the tracks of many animals and birds. Meadowland will carry evidence of moles busy below the surface and, in January, there is always the opportunity to spot the weasel wearing ermine. Indeed, on the higher ground of East Cheshire, it is just possible to glimpse the mountain hare in its white pelage. The deer, following their autumnal rut, look somewhat jaded and bedraggled.

In former times when our economy was basically rural and most of our ancestors worked on the land, the Christmas seasonal festivities usually extended to Plough Monday, the first Monday after Twelfth Night. This was the day, as its name implies, when work finally re-commenced.

There is nothing unusual about the recent series of mild winters, at least if the weather lore of our forebears is to be taken seriously. The weather has always been variable. As one old saw has it:

"As the days lengthen
So does the cold strengthen."

But, as another piece of folk wisdom tells us:

"A January Spring
is worth nothing".

However, the finest summary of all is perhaps:

"The blackest month in all the year
is the month of Janiveer."

Along the way

From Roman times, perhaps even earlier, the River Dee was a busy, maritime highway with Chester being the major port on the west coast of England. Throughout the medieval period and into Tudor and Stuart times, it was the premier port of embarkation for Ireland. With the introduction of larger vessels and the silting-up of the estuary, Chester declined. Attempts to retain this lucrative trade led to the construction of ports along the western shoreline of the Wirral, notably at Neston and Parkgate but, in turn, these declined, sea-going traffic being transferred to the new, growing port of Liverpool on the neighbouring estuary of the Mersey.

Today the estuary of the River Dee has extensive mud flats spread over more than 32,000 acres, mostly covered with grass and other vegetation. It presents the appearance of a wild, windswept expanse with an atmosphere of extensive space where ever-changing light creates a haunting beauty of its own. It is best visited in winter when the silence is occasionally broken by the melancholic, almost plaintive calling of the curlew or plover as it rises from the wilderness of the marshes before the incoming tide. On a clear day of winter sunlight, the Welsh shoreline, five miles away, is visible with the snow-capped Moel Famau in the Clwydian Hills easy to identify.

During the autumn and winter months these mud flats and sandbanks, rich in invertebrate life, become the feeding grounds for thousands of wading birds including sanderling, plovers, bar-tailed godwits, knot, lapwing and turnstone. The ideal time to visit is between one hour before and one hour after high tide when enormous flocks rise into the air and wheel round in dense clouds as they move closer inshore before the advancing waters. It is during this period that they are vulnerable to the attacks of hen harrier, merlin and sparrowhawk.

There is also a resident population of oystercatcher, grey heron, shelduck, teal, wigeon, tufted duck and pochard, supplemented by such hedgerow species as chaffinch, goldfinch, titmice and blackbird.

It is possible to purchase copies of the current tide-tables from the Visitor Centre, Station Road, Thurstaston, Wirral. Phone: 0151 648 4371.

Willaston

The earliest recorded mention of Willaston dates from 1230 when the village gave its name to the Hundred of Wilaveston or Wirral. Therefore, the Hundred Court, the main administrative centre for the entire peninsula, was located there. One of the most fascinating buildings is Willaston Hall with its Elizabethan facade although several substantial seventeenth and eighteenth century farmhouses are to be discovered in the village and its surrounds.

The village focuses on the half-timbered inn, which dates from the reign of Charles I. Overlooking the Green, this was, until recently, the venue for the Boxing Day meet of the Royal Rock Beagles, reputedly the oldest pack in England. Surprisingly for a village of such antiquity, the church is of nineteenth century date although it is distinguished by its bellcot and steeply pitched roof.

Willaston windmill, the tallest in the Wirral, dates from 1800 and in its heyday provided employment for 40 people. Now minus sails, it has been converted into a private residence, having served as a look-out post for the Home Guard during the Second World War.

The railway, a single track from Hooton to West Kirby, reached Willaston and its station in Hadlow Road in 1866, thereby providing local farmers with swift access to Liverpool and Chester for the sale of milk directly to the general public. However, the surplus was still converted to cheese until recent times. Today most of Willaston's inhabitants are commuters working in either Ellesmere Port, Liver-

Hadlow Road Station

pool or Chester.

Little Neston

The Old Quay, the remains of which are visited on this walk, was once a point of embarkation for Ireland and was often used by smugglers or by Irish immigrants making their way to Chester and other

English towns. Swiss Cottage, the tall house at the end of the village, is the one where Lady Hamilton was born. Her father was the village blacksmith. One of the surprises is that during the early years of the twentieth century the largest employer in Little Neston was the colliery, which was located on the coast. Its closure in 1926 resulted in serious unemployment in the area.

Parkgate

The small resort of Parkgate derives its name from Neston Park which was enclosed for hunting about 1250. It served as a deer park for approximately 350 years. As the port of Chester declined it was superseded by Parkgate until, it, too, was doomed by the silting-up of the Dee Estuary. The village was firmly established as a port by 1720 and for the next century was renowned as the terminal for the packet ships which carried passengers to Dublin. The large black and white house, now Mostyn House School, was formerly the hotel where Handel is reputed to have stayed whilst waiting to embark *en route* for Dublin and the very first public performance of "The Messiah".

Parkgate had little chance of surviving as a port after 1815 when the River Dee was artificially diverted to flow along the Welsh coastline. For a time it became a fashionable resort but its present tourist trade is mainly confined to day trippers who appreciate the high quality of the shell fish on sale in the fish shops. The Promenade offers a fine view out over the mud flats to the Welsh shore.

Gayton Sands

The RSPB reserve at Gayton Sands which covers some 5,000 acres, is a wildlife site of international importance protected by the Ramsar Convention, an international agreement drawn up at Ramsar in Iran to safeguard wetland sites considered to be of international importance for wildlife and ratified by the British government in 1976. Throughout the winter months it enjoys one of the largest aggregations of ducks and wading birds in the British Isles including 7,000 shelduck, and 11,000 pintail. In addition there are large populations of mallard, teal, wigeon, red-breasted merganser, oystercatcher, grey plover, redshank, knot and dunlin. These, and the flocks of finches and buntings, attract the attention of such raptors as the merlin, peregrine falcon and short-eared owl.

The Wirral Way

The Wirral Way or the Wirral Country Park, the first to be created in England in the 1960s, follows the line of the former single track railway which ran from Hooton to West Kirby. This was operated jointly by the Great Western Railway Company and the London, Midland and Scottish. It was a well patronised route used by business men heading for Liverpool and also by schoolchildren and day trippers on their way to Parkgate.

Goods traffic consisted principally of coal from Neston Colliery and farm produce, especially milk. With the closure of the colliery and the advent of the car the decline of the railway was inevitable. The last passenger train ran in September, 1956, with the final goods train operating in 1962.

The most important surviving feature of the railway is the station at Hadlow Road, Willaston, which still retains the appearance it had in the 1950s. This is now used as the Visitor Centre.

Route Directions

Leave the car park at Hadlow Road by heading westwards towards the station buildings. As signed, turn left onto the platform and then right, continuing for the full length to pass through the cream-coloured wooden kissing gate at the far end. Cross directly over Hadlow Road itself to continue along the Wirral Way which, at this point, is lined with leafless silver birch, hawthorn and other trees. In late January the snowdrops are often in flower.

The former railway line passes through a flat, pastoral landscape, initially with paddocks on the right and the occasional glimpse of the snow-covered Clwydian Hills in the far distance away to the left. After approximately a quarter of a mile pass to the left of a large pond graced with moorhen and the first of several large patches of gorse, already in flower. The trunks of several of the adjacent trees are festooned with climbing ivy.

Within a further 500 metres negotiate a wooden barrier and, 100 metres beyond, pass beneath the arched red sandstone bridge which

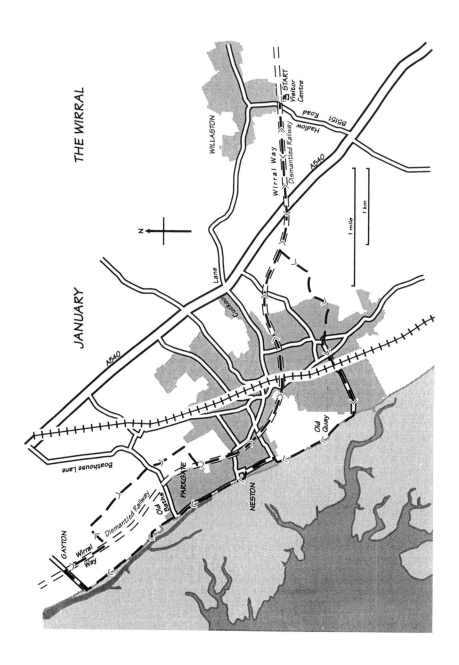

carries Damhead Lane overhead. Within a further short distance the Wirral Way goes under the A540, carried by a concrete bridge. At the far end of this bear right to walk alongside a wooden fence and remain directly ahead until ten metres beyond a bridge with wooden railings.

There, by the sign reading, "Cuckoo Lane to Little Neston", turn left and descend the railway embankment by steps to reach a wooden stile. Turn right along Cuckoo Lane which, in winter, can be exceptionally muddy. Initially the lane climbs between the holly hedges to gain an altitude of 63 metres, the highest point along the entire route.

At the summit, with a stile on your left and facing a five-barred gate, turn right, still following Cuckoo Lane and continue until emerging onto Gorstons Lane in Little Neston. Turn left and, having passed Woodfall Lane Junior School, take the first turn right into Woodfall Lane. At the subsequent junction turn right, briefly, into School Lane and, at the next junction, by "Cockle Cottage", bear left down Bull Hill.

At the intersection with Burton Road cross directly, thereby maintaining the same direction into Marshlands Road. Pass under the railway bridge and continue for the full length of Marshlands Road until reaching the shore of the River Dee.

Turn right through wooden posts and take the wide track until it is blocked by a five-barred metal gate. Keep to the left of this and, walking between a row of hawthorn trees on your right and the shoreline and marshes on your left, follow the clear path for more than half a kilometre. Where the path curves to the right, stay to the left of a low wall to reach a step stile which provides access to the site of the Old Quay with its substantial stone remains.

You may add an extra dimension to your walk by pausing awhile amongst these ruins and letting your imagination come into play. Think of the sailing ships from all four corners of the globe that once berthed here to discharge and load their cargoes. In those days it would have been a busy, bustling spot enlivened by the creaking of ships' timbers, the rumble of cart wheels and the raucous calls of the dockers. Today, it is a scene of absolute peace and tranquillity. The remains of the port are surrounded by green fields and, where the

River Dee once flowed, there is nothing but a sea of grass and reeds where flocks of goldfinch and other birds roost.

Follow the path through the substantial stone ruins. Cross a wooden footbridge before passing close by a large, square, upright stone, somewhat larger than a gatepost. Stay forward to an obvious gap between two hawthorn trees flanked by gorse bushes and head towards the wooden stile now visible directly ahead.

Stay along the narrow path which clings close to the fence on your right until, after almost a kilometre and facing a bungalow, it swings to the right to emerge into a modern housing estate by Old Quay Close. Almost at once turn left along Manorial Road, ignoring the fact that it is signed as a cul-de-sac. At the far end, where the met- alled surface terminates, continue forward along the path signed "To The Parade". After 100 metres this widens into an unadopted road.

By a large black and white house turn right to reach a T-junction. There, turn left along Hunter's Close and, with the cricket ground on your right, advance to meet Station Road, opposite a facing row of fishermen's cottages. Turn left for 100 metres before making a right turn along The Parade, soon passing the imposing black and white frontage of Mostyn House School which is followed by the shops and cafes of the small resort of Parkgate.

At the far end of The Parade, where the road bends sharply to the right, continue forward, stay to the right of the Boat House Hotel and, after approximately 150 metres, pass, on your left, the car park and picnic area. These were created on the site of the Parkgate Old Baths to serve the RSPB's Gayton Sands Reserve.

Keeping a sharp eye open for all those wading birds, maintain a northerly direction with the silted-up River Dee on your left. The course of the river is an apparently endless mass of grass and reed. Do not attempt to walk on this because it is full of quicksand and riven by numerous hidden water courses. Stay with the path which is clear and easy to follow.

By the far end of the car park and picnic area ignore a Wirral Way sign on your right, instead pass through the wooden kissing gate to stay alongside the estuary with a good, wide path running along the top of a walled embankment. Initially there is a hedge on your right beyond which lies open country but this is soon replaced by a golf course.

Continue for approximately one mile until the path curves to the right alongside a wooden fence. Descend a short flight of steps to meet the end of Gayton Lane. Proceed along this surfaced road for approximately 500 metres first with Gayton Cottage on your left and then passing the ends of Cottage Drive East and Cottage Drive West. Climb slightly to cross a former railway bridge.

Some 30 metres beyond this and by a wooden five-barred gate, turn left through a gap alongside a Wirral Way sign and double back for some 25 metres to meet the disused railway track that forms the Wirral Way. Turn left.

After a considerable distance and having negotiated a gap in a wooden barrier, the Wirral way dips into a shallow hollow and climbs again to cross a wide track linking two sections of the golf course, one on either side of the walking trail. One hundred metres beyond this intersection, and with two wooden five-barred gates flanking both sides of the track, turn left through a waymarked wooden kissing gate.

Follow the clear, waymarked path over the links, staying between two lines of thin blue poles. Climb gradually through a line of trees and to the left of a solitary sandstone gatepost before ascending a flight of three steps on the boundary of the golf course.

At the top turn right to follow a distinct path through a belt of trees but, after 100 metres, swing to the right over a planked foot-bridge before turning sharply to the left and proceeding along the boundary of the golf course.

There is a fence and a hedge on your left which is matched, on your right, by a fine perspective over the Dee Estuary to the Welsh hills. The grassy path makes for excellent walking.

Negotiate a waymarked ladder stile before continuing along the obvious path over the centre of a field to reach a footbridge with a stile at either end. Over this climb to the left of a fence for some 50 metres to a small wooden gate.

Through this continue for a further 50 metres along a wide track to a black and white wooden five-barred gate and then maintain di-rection, staying to the left of the red sandstone wall which forms the boundary of Backwood Hall, a farm on your right. Remain with this track, which soon develops into a hedged lane, until it meets Boathouse Lane by a footpath finger post.

Exercising extreme caution because of fast-moving traffic, cross directly into Wood Lane. Remain along this for some distance until meeting Brook Lane which comes in from your left. About 100 metres beyond this junction turn right through waymarked wooden posts onto a fenced path. A few yards before a bridge which spans the path, veer right up another path which leads to the Wirral Way after some 10 metres.

Turn left along the Wirral Way and proceed over the bridge. Where the Wirral Way appears to reach a dead-end, turn left through a wooden barrier and then turn right to arrive at a five-barred gate after a further 100 metres. This provides an exit onto Station Road, Parkgate.

Turn right for a few metres. Pass the Parkgate village sign and the Conservation Area sign with its full-rigged sailing ship and then make a left turn by the Wirral Way Country Park sign to re-join the Wirral Way.

At the top of the approach road to the former Parkgate railway station, where the surfaced road bends sharply to the left towards the toilet block, stay forward through a wooden barrier. Initially there are tennis courts on your right before the track pursues its course between birch and other deciduous trees. It passes under an arched bridge and through another wooden barrier before reaching a wooden finger post indicating a path to the Old Quay at Neston. This goes off to the right. Ignore it, instead continue along the Wirral Way by passing through yet another wooden barrier.

The route is still fringed by trees, with wood pigeons and jays calling from the bare branches. After some distance the route descends a stepped slope to meet Bridge Street by a demolished bridge. Unfortunately there are no Wirral Way signs to guide you along this exceptionally busy road junction and bend so extra care is necessary.

Turn left for a few metres and then cross Bridge Street to the far pavement and, by a small traffic island, almost immediately turn right into Station Road. After 150 metres pass under a high railway bridge which has a concrete parapet supported by red sandstone columns. Continue along Station Road, lined with residential property, for several hundred metres until reaching a T-junction where Station Road meets a facing road at the point where Bushell Road becomes Medlock Lane.

Cross directly into the facing wide track which is signed as the Wirral Way. This runs for more than half a kilometre through a deep cutting flanked by rock walls some 30 metres high. In winter it is a dark and gloomy place where little light filters through. The canopy of trees consists of sycamore, birch, oak and other deciduous trees, all skeletal in appearance at this season of the year. Some trunks, rooted in the rock face and forcing their way out through the cracks, have contorted themselves into weird shapes as they have grown upwards in search of light. The brambles, ferns and ivy cascade down the rock face. The surface of the track is almost always muddy.

Pass beneath a stone arched bridge high above, before walking beneath another, lower, stone arched bridge which carries Lees Lane over the former railway. Pass to the right of another car park and picnic site before passing through open countryside. After a waymarked gateway, the track again becomes enclosed by trees before reaching the wooden bridge spanning Cuckoo Lane. From this point retrace your outward steps along the Wirral Way until reaching Hadlow Road Station in Willaston.

February

Macclesfield Forest

One of the most breathtaking walks in this collection, it climbs steeply through the dense forest to emerge onto a high plateau of rolling and sweeping moorland before ascending the rocky summit of Shutlingsloe at 506 metres above sea level, the second highest point in Cheshire. The return is across open moorland and through more dense forest.

Route: Trentabank Reservoir – Nessit Hill – Shutlingsloe – Buxtors Hill – Ferriser – Standing Stone – Trentabank Reservoir.

Terrain: A mixture of woodland and moorland paths, some sections upgraded to combat erosion. One stretch is flagged while others may be extremely muddy. There is more than a kilometre of bridleway.

Start: Car park, Trentabank Reservoir, Macclesfield Forest. Map reference: 962712.

Distance: 5½ miles (8.8 kilometres).

Map: "The Peak District: White Peak Area". No. 24 in the OS Outdoor Leisure series.

Public Transport: None to the start of the walk. Daily buses except Sundays from Macclesfield to Langley, one mile from the start.

By Car: The best approach is from the A523. Approximately one mile south of Macclesfield town centre turn into Byrom's Lane, which is signed to Langley and Wincle. Follow the signs to Langley and continue beyond to Leathers Smithy pub. There fork right alongside Ridgegate Reservoir and continue along the road until reaching the car park and Visitor Centre at Trentabank Reservoir.

Refreshments: None along the route but meals available at Leathers Smithy pub approximately one kilometre from the start.

The Month

In common with January, the name February has reached modern English by way of Middle English and French from the Latin. It derives from Februa, the name of a purification feast held in this particular month. This link is still maintained in the Christian calendar,

Candlemas or the Feast of the Purification of Our Lady being celebrated on February 2nd. Church services were once renowned for
the large numbers of candles burned during the ecclesiastical ceremonies. The ringing of church bells was almost universal throughout Western Europe and the day was associated in many places by
the holding of fairs.

In Cheshire, Shropshire and other counties along the Welsh Border it was customary to "purify" the home by placing a bunch of
snowdrops inside. Often called "Candlemas Bells", snowdrops were
believed to flower on February 2nd, as a traditional folk song re-
veals:

"The snowdrop in fairest white array
First rears her head on Candlemas Day"

Until recent times it was customary for Cheshire farmers to take over
the tenancy of their farms on Candlemas Day.

Undoubtedly the most popular of the month's saints is St Valentine, patron of lovers, whose feast falls on the 14th February. Identi-
fication of the holy man is well nigh impossible although two
possible candidates were a priest executed in Rome on the 14th February, 269, and another Valentine, a bishop, executed on the same
date in the year 273.

Tradition in this country claims that this is the date on which
birds chose their mate for the season. Research has shown that certainly the blackbird, missel thrush and partridge do pair during the
month and the second half of February does see an increase in the
amount of bird song. It is quite common to spot birds flying with
nesting material protruding from their beaks as they start to prepare
in earnest for the breeding season.

The snowdrop is far from being the only flower to add a little welcome colour to the countryside at this time of year. The crocus with
its flowers of several hues is a definite eye-catcher, as is the ground
ivy with its purple petals. Less noticeable is the butterbur which
flowers in February well in advance of the appearance of its rhubarb-like leaves. Although the countryside in general may still appear stark and drab, the buds of many trees, particularly hawthorn,
hazel and silver birch are beginning to swell and show the initial
signs of green.

The weather in February can be as variable as any month of the year. This is evident not only from official records but also from popular sayings and beliefs handed down from one generation to another.

The most famous of all is "February fill dike" but, although traditionally it is an exceptionally wet month, it has to be noted that February 1891 was the driest month ever recorded in 233 years of official statistics. It was also very warm with the temperature occasionally exceeding 18C. The February of 1998 almost, but not quite, equalled it. This may be ideal for the walker but certainly not for farmers, as other old saws claim:

"If in February, there be no rain,
"Tis neither good for hay nor grain."
"February's flood does good".
"All the months in the year
Curse a fair Februeer".
"Much February snow
A fine summer doth show."

Along the way

Macclesfield Forest

The original Forest of Macclesfield, consisting principally of native deciduous trees, was declared a hunting area during the eleventh century by Hugh Lupus, the first Earl of Chester, and it continued to be used as such until comparatively modern times.

The principal quarry was wild boar and deer, whose descendants still roam the area although they are seen infrequently. Following the Enclosure Act of 1804 most of the trees were felled, the land being subdivided by drystone walls and used for either sheep or dairy farming. Coniferous trees were planted extensively following the construction of Trentabank Reservoir, mainly to prevent erosion. The most common species of tree to be found in the modern forest are Larch, Sitka Spruce and Lodgepole Pine although in more recent years areas of beech and sycamore have been planted.

In medieval times, the administrative centre for the area was the Chamber in the Forest. The exact location of this building has never been identified although it must have been impressive for it is said to have had sufficient stabling for 600 horses. The Church or the Chapel in the Forest, the present structure dating from 1673 although re-built in 1834, may have stood close to the site of the Chamber.

A school has existed there since 1728 but a century later the parsonage became the schoolmaster's house and lessons were more regular. The number of pupils on the roll varied between 30 and 60 and many had to walk several miles to school "carrying jars of stew and rice pudding over their shoulders." When the Water Authority took over the area for the construction of the reservoirs, they shut down a number of farms and the school attendance declined until it finally closed its doors in 1960.

Buried at Forest Chapel is the Reverend Gage Earle who did so much to revive the sport of falconry. He was vicar from 1856 until 1889. He hawked grouse on the surrounding moors with peregrine falcons and hunted rabbits with goshawks.

An annual rush-bearing ceremony is held at Forest Chapel on the first Sunday after the Glorious Twelfth of August because at that time of year the Earl of Derby was always in residence at Crag Hall for the grouse-shooting season.

Trentabank Reservoir

The heronry located in the larch trees at the eastern end of Trentabank Reservoir is one of the largest, if not the largest in Cheshire. It is indisputably the largest in the Peak District National Park. From mid-February onwards the nesting birds congregate and their harsh croaking calls disturb the silence of the forest. As they drop down through the trees to collect twigs, they may easily be observed from the short wheelchair trail, which runs from the Visitor Centre alongside the reservoir. Their nests are large, rough-looking affairs which appear to perch precariously amongst the higher reaches of the pine trees.

There is a strong probability that during February you may encounter snow on this particular walk for the hills of Macclesfield Forest are often white when other areas of the county are blissfully unaware of the worst of the winter weather. Therefore, it is a good

Trentabank Reservoir

season for looking for the tracks of the deer, stoats, weasels, squirrels and mice that inhabit the Forest and the higher moorlands. In February, too, the larch trees will be brown and bare, having shed their needles the previous autumn but many of the other coniferous trees will still be green.

Built in 1929, Trentabank Reservoir is one of a series in Macclesfield Forest, the others being situated further down the Bollin Valley towards and beyond the village of Langley. Holding some 130 million gallons of water, it supplies the town of Macclesfield and helps to control the flow of water in the River Bollin which has its source in the Forest. In recent years, in co-operation with the Peak District National Park and Macclesfield Borough Council, North West Water PLC has built a Visitor Centre which, being constructed of wood, blends perfectly with the surroundings. It houses displays on the water supply and the local flora and fauna, while the wardens are on hand, especially at weekend, to dispense advice on local walks.

Standing Stone

Approximately half way along this route is a small car park at Standing Stone. Although several finger posts point to this spot, no actual stone is visible. The name derives from not one but five gravestones, now covered with earth and grass. These are reputed to mark the last resting place of people who, for one reason or another, did not "die a Christian death". In previous centuries hanged felons and suicides, for instance, fell into this category and, consequently were denied burial in ground that had not been consecrated.

There is also a strong oral tradition that Shutlingsloe and nearby Wildboarclough were notorious centres of witchcraft. Folk lore also claims that both were places where ancient cults were perpetuated. People who dabbled in such unorthodox or devilish practices were also forbidden a Christian burial. Another possibility is that the graves were those of plague victims.

Perhaps at one time the stones stood upright, but their location is over the wall on your left after you have negotiated the first stile from the road.

By the roadside near Standing Stone car park is a plaque mounted on a large gritstone boulder. It is dedicated to the memory of Walter Smith, 1872 to 1949, who is described as "Historian of Macclesfield"

He was a most unusual man yet typical of so many others of his period who were driven by an insatiable thirst for knowledge even though they had been denied a formal education. After 50 years working on the railway, he retired in 1937 but then started to learn Greek. He was also a local councillor.

His historical research was developed through an extensive knowledge of his native area gained by exploring the hills on foot. His articles on the social history of the district were serialised in a large number of articles in the "Macclesfield Courier". He was a close friend of another local historian, Raymond Richards of Gawsworth Hall, who said of him, "His tall, distinguished figure was often to be seen striding out across the hills to the east of Maccles-field."

Wildboarclough

One of the most notable events in the recorded history of Wildboarclough occurred on the 24th May, 1989 when there was a sudden and unexpected cloudburst on the moors surrounding the Cat and Fiddle and Shining Tor. Clough Brook, which runs through the valley, was unable to cope with the vast torrent of water, which suddenly rushed off the hills.

Roads, bridges and footpaths were washed away. Stone walls crumbled and trees were torn from the ground and carried along by the flood waters. Cattle were swept down the valley. The post box has never been found. The floods caused damage in excess of one millions pounds.

In the fifteenth century, the land in and around Wildboarclough was owned by the Stanley family. Then it was used mainly for hunting and is one of many places in England which claims the privilege of being the one where the last wild boar was shot.

However, the abundance of fast flowing streams to provide water power brought the Industrial Revolution which saw the opening of calico printing works, the Crag Works. The Earl of Derby built Crag Hall for his local residence and a row of cottages for his workers.

The advent of steam power led to the closure of the enterprise in 1860 and Wildboarclough again became an agrarian community. The works were restored for use as a workshop, store-house and office for the Derby Estate. It later housed the local post office, said to be the largest sub post office in Britain. Parts were later demolished and it is now a private residence.

The emphasis on sheep farming is summarised by the local rhyme;

> *"There once was a man from the Clough*
> *Who said, 'I've had quite enough!*
> *From Wincle to Sutton*
> *There's nothing but mutton,*
> *And I'm heartily sick of the stuff! "*

Route Directions

Leave the car park by passing to the left of the Visitor Centre and Picnic Area. Immediately through a wooden gate cross a rough track and continue ahead with a fence and the road on your left until reaching a wooden kissing gate. Do not negotiate this. Rather, bear right by the wooden finger post to begin climbing the broad track signed to Shutlingsloe. There is a wall on your right and trees on your left.

The path, improved and re-surfaced in recent years, climbs steeply with occasional glimpses of Trentabank Reservoir through the trees to your left. Although the forest is predominantly composed of coniferous trees, the path itself is fringed with oaks, rowan, beech and other deciduous trees.

Where the wall on the right terminates there is a seat and a platform for viewing the heronry down below. On reaching a three-armed finger post just beyond ignore the path leading off to the right. Instead continue upwards with the main path, which is now even wider with another wall on the right.

After a further 200 metres, where this second wall comes to an end, the path curves sharply to the left. The forest closes in on both sides, the ground to the left falling away steeply and that to the right climbing, also very steeply. For a short distance the gradient eases considerably before increasing dramatically until reaching another wooden seat, thoughtfully and kindly provided by North West Water PLC, the owners of the land and the forest.

Afterwards the going eases and although by no means level, the path rises to reach a wooden kissing gate adjacent to a wooden five-barred gate. Ten metres beyond this comes a junction of paths with a finger post. Ignore the bridleway running-off to the right and signed, "To Trentabank via Nessit Hill". Remain with the broad track as it bends to the left and the going levels for a short distance before resuming its steep upwards course to another junction with another finger post.

Here, turn right along the narrower path signed to Shutlingsloe. Climb by yet another seat on the right and exit the forest for the first views of open country. These include the sweeping vista of High Moor, looking towards Oakenclough, and the tree-covered Nessit Hill.

One hundred metres beyond this seat another junction is reached which is recognisable by a Macclesfield Forest Information board. Here, make a right turn through a wooden kissing gate, with a Peak and Northern Footpath Society sign which reads, "To Wildboarclough via Shutlingsloe Farm and To Langley."

This new path is partially flagged and, in one or two places, stepped. The higher it climbs the wider the views which now embrace Shutlingsloe, directly ahead, Croker Hill with its radio mast, the Cheshire Plain, Jodrell Bank and, on a clear day, the Welsh Hills away to the right. To the left they include the Cat and Fiddle, Shining Tor, the highest point in the county, Cats Tor, Axe Edge and, in the far distance, more of the Peak District moorlands.

This section of the route used to be extremely boggy but the flags and a short stretch of duck boarding make for easier and definitely pleasanter walking, the improvements having blended in with the immediate surroundings.

At the far end of the duck boarding there is a stile with another Peak and Northern Footpath Society alongside. Over the stile turn sharply to the right, taking the more obvious of the two paths indicated. Walk closely to the wall on your right for 500 metres to gain a stone step stile set into the facing wall.

Beyond climb the steep set of stone steps, former gravestones, to find the Triangulation Pillar on the summit of Shutlingsloe at 506 metres or 1,657 feet above sea level. This is one of the finest viewpoints in the entire Peak District National Park and certainly the best in the entire county of Cheshire.

In addition to the landmarks and features cited above, from here it is possible to gaze down directly into Wildboarclough, a verdant oasis surrounded by high, brooding and rolling moorlands. In February, they are often covered with a thick blanket of snow, only the occasional dry stone wall adding a touch of black to the landscape. In addition you can also see the Roaches, Hen Cloud and Tittesworth Reservoir, all in Staffordshire.

On the summit there is a memorial plaque to the memory of Arthur Smith, a ceaseless campaigner for footpaths and open access. It was erected here several years ago by the Peak and Northern Footpath Society and the Ramblers' Association when his ashes were scattered from the summit, a ceremony which was broadcast by the BBC.

From the summit retrace your route down the stone steps, over the step stile and alongside the wall to the wooden stile with the Peak and North sign alongside. There, turn left, re-cross the duck boarding and follow the flagged path to the wooden gate with another sign adjacent.

Through this a junction is reached with the Macclesfield Forest Information Panel. Leave your outward route at this point by turning

FEBRUARY   MACCLESFIELD FOREST

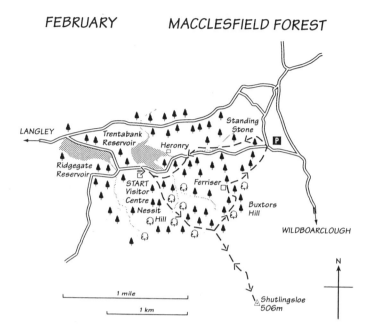

right along a very narrow path for some 50 metres until reaching a bridleway. Turn right again to walk through the forest on a broad track which undulates and snakes gently. Where the bridleway bends through 90 degrees to the left there is a short flight of facing steps followed by a path running to the immediate right of a stone wall. *Ignore this path.*

Instead remain along the bridleway as indicated by the adjacent finger post which reads, "Forest Walks 2, 3." A short distance beyond pass to the left of "Ferriser", a farm which was abandoned when the area was first used as a water catchment zone. Still standing firmly, its windows and doors have been sealed up, although its outbuildings have been allowed to fall into ruin.

Eventually the forest on the right comes to an end and there are further views of the Cat and Fiddle and surrounding moors. A newly-excavated pond, with a solitary tree rising from the centre, is passed on the left.

Continue along the bridleway until reaching a wooden five-barred gate with a footpath sign reading "Shutlingsloe" is reached. This gate provides an exit onto a junction of three minor roads. One heads for Wildboarclough, another to Macclesfield (5 miles) and a third to Buxton (7 miles).

Continue directly ahead. After 50 metres along the road turn left into Standing Stone car park. Stay with the main entrance drive, walking to the immediate left of a wooden fence. After 50 metres turn right through a small wooden kissing gate and then make an immediate left turn to a waymarker post showing two Forest Walks.

Maintain direction taking the path signed with the number 2 waymarker. Initially the path is grassy and to the right of a stone wall, immediately beyond which is the minor road descending steeply to Trentabank Reservoir.

The rapidly descending path passes through a stone gateway and then, losing its grassy surface, winds its way deeper into the forest as it continues to lose altitude, sometimes rapidly, sometimes more gradually, until, eventually, its forms a T-junction with a forest ride. Ignoring the waymark, turn left for some 5 metres to a stile and finger post.

Turn right along the narrow road for 200 metres to another finger post which reads, "Trentabank". Turn left through the gap stile and then immediately right. After 20 metres veer left over Bollin Brook, culverted at this point, and then right again so that the path runs along the left bank of the brook.

Climb and descend sets of steps, re-cross the stream by a wooden footbridge and remain along the clear path through the trees until meeting a gap stile alongside another finger post, this time pointing to Standing Stone.

Emerge onto the road and turn left, using the well-trodden path running along the grass verge as it rounds the head of Trentabank Reservoir before running along its southern flank.

On reaching the lay-by with its display panel illustrating the range of bird species to be observed there, cross the road, climb the bank and turn right to stride out along the path signed to Shutlingsloe as it runs to the left of a fence. After 50 metres pass through a wooden kissing gate and, ignoring the path to the left, again signed to Shutlingsloe, maintain direction along the track heading for Trentabank. After 100 metres pass through a small wooden gate and continue forward, passing to the right of the Visitor Centre for the car park.

March

Swettenham

A gentle walk in Central Cheshire to see the daffodils at their best.

Route: Brereton Heath Country Park – Davenport House – Swettenham Church – Daffodil Dell – Ashtree Farm – Swettenham – Brereton Heath Country Park.

Terrain: A mixture of bridleways, tracks, field paths and lanes with a little road walking. An undulating route with several steep but short climbs.

Start: Brereton Heath Country Park. Map reference 795656.

Distance: 8 miles (12½ kilometres). Reduced to 5 miles (8 kilometres) if Daffodil Dell and Quinta Gardens are omitted.

Map: OS Explorer 267 - Northwich & Delamere Forest.

Public Transport: There is a limited daily service to Brereton village from Sandbach and Holmes Chapel. No buses on Sundays.

By Car: Brereton Heath Country Park is signed from the A54 approximately midway between Holmes Chapel and Congleton. If approaching from Congleton turn left for approximately a quarter of a mile. There is a pay and display car park, Visitor Centre and toilets.

Refreshments: Bar meals and restaurant at the Swettenham Arms, lunch-time and evenings.

The Month

The name "March" is derived from Mars, the Roman god of war. In his play "Julius Caesar" Shakespeare has given English literature one of its most famous lines, "Beware the Ides of March", the Ides being the fifteenth day of the month. More importantly, perhaps, the 21st March is the date of the Spring Equinox when, for the first time in the year, the hours of daylight exceed those of darkness. Therefore, it is a turning point, a time of optimism which signals that Winter is behind us and Summer is an approaching prospect.

Despite this the weather is definitely unreliable. Gales are a common occurrence, rainfall may be heavy but, usually there are contrasting days of bright sunshine and the temperature is definitely rising.

In response to seasonal triggers the hedgerows acquire a dusting of green as the buds slowly transform themselves into leaves. The larger trees begin to sprout larger buds, occasionally leaves. Before the tree canopy shades out the sunshine the woodland flowers such as wild garlic, wood anemones and primroses burst into bloom to provide the woodland floor with a rich carpet of colour.

Badgers, bats, hedgehogs and other mammals bestir themselves while frogs and toads migrate to their spawning grounds. Over-wintering geese, swans and ducks depart whilst the month may also see the arrival of our first summer migrants. Resident species such as blackbird, thrush, robin, wren and titmice will be on the nest and, if the weather is extremely favourable, may have their first nestlings by the time March draws to a close. The frisky behaviour of the hare is yet another feature of the month.

The 3rd March is the feast day of St Chad who left the Abbey of Lindisfarne in Northumbria to become the first Bishop of Lichfield. Cheshire was an important part of his large diocese which was rather fitting because he did more than any other of the early missionaries to convert the county to Christianity. Cheadle derives its name from "Chad's Hill", the spot close by the Bicker Brook where he baptised his converts. A stone Saxon cross, a relic of those distant days, was discovered just over a century ago buried nearby and is now on display in Abney Hall, Cheadle.

Another reminder of this local saint is to be found in the ancient church of Chadkirk which lies between Romiley and Marple. No longer used for religious services it has been converted into a Visitor Centre serving the local country park.

March weather has generated considerable folklore but perhaps the most famous saying of them all is:

"March winds and April showers
Bring forth May flowers".

Yet another informs us:

"Much March dust and a shower in May
Makes the corn green and the fields gay."

Along the way

Brereton Heath

Brereton Heath once formed part of the vast estates owned by the Brereton family. The land was mainly unproductive and remained as heath and woodland but, following the discovery of vast deposits of silica sand in 1959, large scale quarrying was developed. The topsoil was removed and the sand extracted for more than a decade for use in glass-making, cosmetics and industry. Afterwards it lay dormant until 1981 when Congleton Borough Council bought it for transformation into a country park.

The focal point of this is the large lake which, fringed by willows and other trees, was formed by flooding the former workings. It is the setting for the Dane Valley Willow Project which aims to restore and manage the local willow bed and to revive interest in the traditional skills of basket weaving.

Locally grown willow from the Dane Valley was once woven into baskets for use in the cotton mills of Manchester and Lancashire. As part of this scheme, four artists in residence have created a series of sculptures in willow which form the basis of the Brimstone Trail, a waymarked route which commences in the car park and takes about half an hour to complete.

The lake itself is noted for its population of mute swans, mallard, coot, moorhen and other aquatic birds while, in March, the surrounding woodlands, barely showing the first dusting of green in March, already echo to the song of resident birds including wren, blackbird, robin, wood pigeon, collared dove and the woodpecker.

Swettenham

This charming village in central Cheshire never enjoyed the benefits of the railway age and, consequently, has altered little over the centuries. The focal point is the delightful church of St Peter. Dating from the thirteenth century it occupies the site of an earlier ecclesiastical building. Originally it was half-timbered, as with the church at Marton, but the only reminder of this may still be seen in the north wall. The remainder of the building was enclosed by brick during the early eighteenth century.

It is alleged that St Peter's is connected by an underground tunnel to the Swettenham Arms, said to occupy the site of a former nunnery. There is no real evidence of this although a ghost, said to be that of a nun who was murdered because she broke her vows, used to be seen in the Rectory. She has not been seen since absolution was recited each night for two weeks at the beginning of the twentieth century.

Another ghost is claimed for Swettenham Hall, an ancient manor house. She is a lady dressed all in black who appears to members of the family as an omen of bad times to come.

Swettenham is renowned for its two Gooseberry Shows. On the last Saturday in June only those grown in the village are eligible for entry but, a week later, an open competition is staged. The village has no bus services and no shops but there is a post office located in the little cottage beside the ford. The village school closed in 1969 when the children were transferred to Marton.

Daffodil Dell

Daffodils, thousands of them with their bright yellow heads dancing gently in the breeze, are the main feature of this walk during the second half of March. For many decades, Swettenham has been renowned throughout the county for the fine display which is to be enjoyed in Daffodil Dell, a steep-sided and wooded valley beside Swettenham Mill. The area is blessed with several small waterfalls where side-streams tumble into Swettenham Brook.

The bulbs were originally planted many years ago by Wilfrid Lancaster, a former owner of the mill and additional plantings every year since have not only maintained the tradition but created a golden yellow wonderland as a tribute to Spring. The absence of a woodland canopy at this time of year permits other woodland flowers including anemones, celandine and wild garlic to flower as well. The broad-leaved trees also provide an ideal habitat for numerous species of birds so that a stroll to admire the daffodils is accompanied by a concert of birdsong.

Daffodil Dell is open every day of the year throughout the hours of daylight. There is an admission charge of 50 pence (honesty box).

Daffodil Dell

The money raised is used to maintain the display and to introduce other plants and flowers.

More recent plantings of daffodils by local residents along the roadside verges have perpetuated the custom and many splendid clusters may be seen as you stroll through the village. In Swettenham Cemetery, a small semi-circle of public grassland not far from the church, even more daffodils raise their heads through the turf. A thoughtfully provided bench allows the visitor to sit and admire.

Quinta Gardens

As you enter the village of Swettenham from the direction of Brereton Heath a small wooden kissing gate adjacent to a cattle grid on your left permits access to the Quinta Gardens. Now managed by the Cheshire Wildlife Trust, though not widely publicised, these gardens were developed around his private residence by Sir Bernard Lovell, the astronomer and physicist associated with Jodrell Bank and space exploration by means of radio waves. They form an arboretum offering a mix of indigenous and exotic species of tree collected and assembled from many parts of the world. The various sections reflect the achievements and main events of Sir Bernard's life.

Reith Avenue, predominantly formed by red-twigged lime trees, recall the Reith Lectures, given on BBC Radio by Sir Bernard in 1958. Knight's Avenue, consisting of Lombardy Poplars, was planted to commemorate the granting of his knighthood in 1961. The nearby rhododendron, a native of Szechwan where it grows at an altitude of between 5,000 and 7,000 feet, flowers during February and March. There is also an unusual multi-stemmed Cornell from China as well as several Scots Pines. Jubilee Ride, consisting of Jack Pines grown from seeds collected in Canada, dates from the Queen's Silver Jubilee in 1977.

One of the most unusual items is an Oriental Plane. It is recorded that Hippocrates, the Father of Medicine, always taught his students sitting beneath the shade of an Oriental Plane tree on the Greek island of Cos. The example to be found in the Quinta Gardens was planted by Sir Bernard in 1964 as a seedling given to him by the 6th Earl of Bradford from Weston Park in Shropshire. The tree there, 300 years-old but removed after the gales of 1985, was grown from a seed taken from the Oriental Plane in Cos. This means that the Swettenham plane tree is a direct descendant of the one associated with Hippocrates.

Another delight of the gardens is the Quinta Pond which provides an important habitat for many plants and creatures including the alder fly and the common toad. Two veteran oaks nearby are a remnant from the period when the area was enclosed by hedges and pockets of woodland. At the appropriate season examples of foxglove, hogweed, primrose, blue bell and red campion are to be seen around the fringes of the pond.

Swettenham Meadows

Yet another attraction of this walk is the section between Brereton Heath and Swettenham where the bridleway traverses the valley of the River Dane. The river, which pursues a meandering course through the soft sands and gravels common to this part of Cheshire, is flanked by willows and waterside meadows which produce excellent grazing for the county's famous dairy cattle.

Swettenham Meadows, traversed after the crossing of Midge Brook, are owned and managed by the Cheshire Wildlife Trust, their main attraction being the variety and succession of wild flowers to be found there throughout the summer months.

Route Directions

Leave the car park by the main entrance, turning right by the telephone kiosk to walk along Davenport Lane. Initially there is a mixed deciduous woodland on your immediate right while to the left the landscape is extensive and pastoral. Immediately ahead, in the far distance, is the bowl-shaped landmark of Jodrell Bank radio telescope.

On reaching the A54, the Congleton to Holmes Chapel road, exercise extreme caution in crossing to the signed bridleway immediately facing, its entrance guarded by the unusually shaped and cream-coloured Davenport Lodge. Stay to the right of Grange Farm and then to the left of Davenport House before negotiating a white gate to continue along the neatly fenced track.

At the Y-junction by a pond veer right to meet a second Y-junction after 100 metres. Fork right again to pass a descending series of small pools on the slope to your right. The bridleway twists into the well-wooded Dane Valley, passing a giant oak still clad in the Hovis-brown foliage of the previous autumn, before reaching a stand of weeping willow by the river, their nascent buds creating a shimmering green veil. They are frequented by flocks of long-tailed tits.

Negotiating another small gate, cross the River Dane by a bridge with green metal railings before veering right, still with the track, before passing a cream-coloured house with the intriguing name of "Dragon's Cave".

From this point onwards the lane, hedged with holly and hawthorn and the bright yellow flowers of the lesser celandine adding a welcome dash of colour to the verges, begins to climb until, shortly before entering Swettenham village, acquires a surface. The small, half-moon shaped field, signed as "Swettenham Cemetery" on the right is worth a pause to admire its display of daffodils, a seat being provided for anyone in search of rest or contemplation. Just beyond, but on the left, is the entrance to the Quinta Gardens.

Continue a short way further until reaching St Peter's Church on your left. There, by a footpath sign, turn right over a wooden stile, advancing to a second after a mere 50 metres. Remain to the left of a fence before crossing directly over an open field while aiming for a large, waymarked tree and with a view of Shutlingsloe in the far distance ahead.

Maintain direction to the right of another fence and spasmodic hedge to a stile adjacent to a five-barred gate. Proceed a further 150 metres to another stile, noticing that the hedge remnants were layered by country craftsmen many decades ago. Beyond the next waymarked stile cross a ploughed field to yet another stile before heading for the diametrically opposite corner of the subsequent field where a stile stands by a footpath sign, a water trough and some black and white gates.

Turn left to walk for 12 metres between white railings flanking the drive to Swettenham Hall before reaching the junction formed by Congleton Road and Swettenham Lane opposite the Swettenham Club. Go across the entrance to Swettenham Lane before turning left along Congleton Road. Descend a few metres to cross Swettenham brook. The mill and entrance to Daffodil Dell are on your right. After visiting the Dell, a gentle stroll of approximately one kilometre in each direction, resume walking along the road, climbing steeply for approximately 100 metres.

Immediately round the first bend turn sharp left into the lane, recognised by a notice announcing, **"DEEP FORD AHEAD"**. Proceed along this lane but, by Brookhouse Farm, veer right along the specially constructed pathway over a stone-slabbed bridge which enables pedestrians to avoid the actual ford. Afterwards climb steeply for approximately 200 metres until meeting the road. Turn right for a further 200 metres and, by a footpath sign, go right over a wooden stile.

The path is somewhat indistinct so bear diagonally right for 50 metres to a waymarked telegraph pole and then turn left to descend the grass slope to a wooden footbridge spanning the stream as it flows through a tree-filled, steep-sided valley.

MARCH   SWETTENHAM

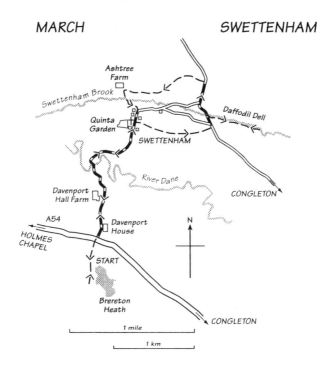

At the far end of the bridge a small notice announces that the next section of the path traverses Swettenham Meadows, a nature reserve owned by the Cheshire Wildlife Trust. In March, it resembles any other nondescript piece of countryside but in summer the meadows produce a succession of wild flowers.

From the end of the footbridge bear right, as directed by a waymark, to follow the clear path as it twists and turns while climbing the slope diagonally to a stile by a telegraph pole, a footpath sign and a wooden gate. Over the stile turn left along another bridleway which is lined with an abundance of bramble. In the far distance is a view of Mow Cop in Staffordshire.

Ignore a path to the right, continuing for half a kilometre until reaching Ash Tree Farm. There, turn left, passing either side of a locked five-barred wooden gate, to walk down an unsigned bridleway which soon crosses the brook before climbing between grass verges. At the top of the hill, and by another footpath sign, turn left along a lane which soon reaches the road by a phone kiosk and pillar box.

Turn right to pass to the left of St Peter's Church and to the right of the Parish School, now a private residence, and so follow the outward route across the Dane Valley back to the car park at Brereton Heath Country Park.

An extra mile around the Brimstone Trail for sightings of such willow sculptures as "The Nest", "The Spiral" and "The Tunnel" will be well rewarded.

April

Gawsworth

A route through gentle, undulating countryside based on one of the county's most historic villages.

Route: Gawsworth – Rodegreen – Manor Farm – North Rode – Macclesfield Canal – Fool's Nook – Mount Farm – Gawsworth.

Terrain: Mainly field paths, canal tow paths and bridleways. Undulating but no serious climbing. May be muddy in places.

Start: By the footpath sign a few yards south-west of Gawsworth Church. Map reference: 888696.

Distance: 7½ miles (12 kilometres).

Map: OS Explorer 268 - Macclesfield & Congleton

Public Transport: Gawsworth is served by frequent daily buses (including Sundays after midday) from Macclesfield, Congleton, Sandbach and Crewe.

By Car: Gawsworth lies on the A536 Macclesfield to Congleton road from which the Hall is signed. It may also be reached by minor roads, signposted, from Marton, Siddington and Monk's Heath, all on the A34 between Alderley Edge and Congleton. It is linked by another minor road to Fool's Nook on the A523 Macclesfield to Leek road. Park on the roadside a few yards south-west of Gawsworth Church.

Refreshments: Bar meals are available at the Fool's Nook Inn, part way through the walk. From the end of June, 2000, the new tea rooms at Gawsworth Hall will be open at the same hours as the Hall. Phone: 01260 223456

The Month

April, which takes its name from the Latin, *Aprilis*, is the fourth month of the year with Spring well and truly established. Not only are the hours of daylight much longer but, with the clocks having gone forward, the evenings themselves are extended so that by the end of the month short walks are possible after work.

The resident bird population is augmented by the first summer migrants as we listen for the first evocative call of the cuckoo which, on the eastern moorlands of the county fosters its offspring notably on the meadow pipit. Swallows, swifts, chiffchaff, willow warbler and other birds also arrive.

Florally it is the prime time for all those woodland species which flower before the summer canopy of the trees blots out all the sunlight. It is a delight to wander through woodlands carpeted with wild garlic, anemones and celandine. The hedgerows are at their best, not only with the bright green foliage but full of nesting birds. Hedgerow flowers, too, make their appearance, the grass verges sporting vivid and colourful displays of daisies and dandelions and, if the weather is kind, the first of the season's red campion and ragwort.

As for the mammal populations, the hedgehogs come out of hibernation while the late-night or early morning walker may well catch glimpses of the badger or the vixen with her latest cubs. The number of mole hills always appears to increase.

In most years April sees the first of the Bank Holidays, Easter, which provides a week-end to be savoured in the countryside, whether on high moorlands or the gentler gradients of the pastoral plains.

Easter apart, the month has several notable festivals. It is inaugurated by April Fools' Day, which needs no explanation. The 23rd is the feast of England's patron, St George, although his associations with this country are negligible. He was an officer serving under the Roman Emperor Diocletian. In the year 300 he was put to death for refusing to abandon his Christian faith. His associations with the dragon are probably pure mythology and his adoption as the English patron saint appears to date from the time of the Crusades. Later, St George's Chapel, Windsor, was founded and the "St George" is the badge of the Order of the Garter which was established by King Edward III.

In medieval times many towns and cities, including Chester, held special ceremonies in his honour, even erecting equestrian statues for the day. Until 1811, the annual Chester race meeting on the Roodee was invariably held on the Feast of St George.

In 1609 Robert Amery of Chester had three silver cups made which were to be competed for in the "St George's Race" held every

year on the Roodee on the 23rd April. In the early years of the following century the race was transferred to the course at Farndon.

The final day of the month was celebrated in Cheshire, as elsewhere in the country, as May-Day Eve. It was the practice to fasten
May birches over doorways and fireplaces. These were intended to
convey a compliment. Often hawthorn was used but if the chosen
branches were alder, pronounced locally as "owler", it signified that
the occupant of the premises was a "scowler".

In popular belief April was invariably associated with showers of
rain and this has been encapsulated in folklore, much of it universally throughout the country:

"A cold April
The barn will fill."

Or, alternatively:

"A cold April
Gives bread and wine."

Yet another old saw informs us that

"When April blows his horn
It is good for hay and corn."

Or:

Better an April sop than a May clot."

Along the way

Gawsworth Village

Undoubtedly it is the tranquil setting which creates the beauty and
appeal of Gawsworth village. The church of St James, surrounded by
tall trees, reflects in the lake which forms the foreground to the ancient Hall. The Old Rectory, timber-framed, stands across the road
facing the church while the New Rectory, dating from 1707, is to be
found adjacent to the churchyard. Also facing the lake is the New
Hall, also erected in 1707, when it was built for Lord Mohun who,
with his rival the Duke of Hamilton, died in one of the most famous
duels in the history of Cheshire. Their quarrel concerned the
Gawsworth estates.

Gawsworth Hall

The village is featured in the Domesday Book of 1086 as Goursmourde and is believed to occupy the site of a much older Neolithic settlement. The present Hall and church may be on the site of a wooden church and stone manor house where the Orreby family lived when they were granted the manor of Gawsworth for "one caparisoned horse."

The present Hall is a splendid half-timbered Tudor manor house built by the Fitton family who owned the manor for 400 years. They were also responsible for the re-building of the church and landscaping the surrounding parkland which covered several square miles. Four of the original five fish ponds still survive. The coat-of-arms of the Fitton family may still be seen carved on the chimney stacks. Much of the interior of the Hall, including the drawing room, remains more or less in its original condition. Outside, at the rear of the building, is one of the few remaining examples of a medieval jousting ground. Today, on summer evenings, there are open-air concerts, operas and productions of Shakespearean plays.

This is more than appropriate because one of Gawsworth Hall's most famous inhabitants was Mary Fitton, one of the claimants to being the Dark Lady of Shakespeare's sonnets. She was a maid of honour at the court of Elizabeth 1. Another character associated with this corner of Cheshire was Maggoty Johnson, the last professional jester in England who was buried in Maggoty Johnson's Wood in 1773. Now owned by the National Trust, this is located between the Hall and the A536.

The parish church of St James was re-built by the Fittons in the fifteenth century but it was altered considerably during extensive nineteenth century renovations which resulted in the loss of box pews, medieval stained glass and a rood screen.

However, the Church of St James still retains considerable interest including the tombs and effigies of four generations of the Fitton family along with the armorial bearings of 15 ancient Cheshire families which are carved on the tower which, unusually has eight spires and a collection of winged gargoyles.

The nearby pub, the Harrington Arms is a Queen Anne building and, with its cobbled courtyard and old oak bar, has changed little over the intervening three centuries.

Macclesfield Canal

One section of this route follows the tow path of the Macclesfield Canal which runs for some 26 miles from Marple, near Stockport, to Kidsgrove in the Potteries, thereby linking the Peak Forest Canal with the Trent and Mersey. At an altitude of 500 feet (152 metres) above sea level, it has the distinction of being the highest navigable waterway in the country. At Bosley, between Macclesfield and Congleton, it descends some 30 metres through an impressive flight of locks at the bottom of which it is carried over the River Dane by an iron aqueduct designed by Thomas Telford.

North Rode

When the canal reached the village of North Rode in 1820 the locals celebrated the event which was to change their lives by arranging a gigantic ox roast. The parish church is most unusual in having a square tower alongside a round one which creates a most unusual appearance. Although it is built in the Early Norman style it is of comparatively modern origin, having been built in 1846 by the Daintry family.

Until that date, although it merited a mention in Domesday Book, North Rode formed a part of the parish of Prestbury. The industrial history of the village is reflected in such names as Scissorcroft Woods, Weavers' Hey, Brickbank Wood and Kiln Croft. Colley Mill dates back to 1444 while Yew Tree Cottage may be of even greater antiquity.

Route Directions

Facing away from Gawsworth church, and about 100 metres to the south-west, turn left up the short flight of wooden steps by the Peak and Northern Footpath Society sign indicating a route to North Rode. At the top of the grassy bank, negotiate the traditional wooden stile to follow the clear, well-trodden path to the immediate left of a hawthorn hedge, now in full leaf.

The church, with its surrounding trees home to a raucous rookery, is close-by on your left and, much further away in the same direction is the conspicuous radio mast on the summit of Croker Hill.

Over the next stile, in the corner of the field, advance to a waymarked stile with another footpath sign alongside. Cross the next field and, in the far corner, climb another short flight of four steps before negotiating a stile adjacent to a footpath finger post and a holly bush.

On the far side veer slightly leftwards as the path skirts a small lake well patronised by anglers and fringed by reeds and bulrushes. Round the far corner of this lake to another footpath post with a red buoy attached and then bear right to an obvious stile.

Immediately cross a narrow track to a facing stile, with yet another footpath sign adjacent, before continuing forward, now to the right of a hedge until meeting a stile by a very large tree. Beyond, maintain the same direction but now to the right of a fence to gain a stile some 40 metres to the right of the field corner.

Continue along the same bearing but now to the right of a black metal water trough followed by another hedge. Where this curves slightly away stay straight ahead to a stile by a five-barred metal gate, passing one of Cheshire's old marl pits on the way.

Over the stile pass through a belt of trees for 100 metres to a stile alongside a five-barred metal gate with a warped gatepost. Cross another track to a stile within 50 metres and continue alongside a fence and a spasmodic row of trees with Shellow Farm a short distance away to your right.

On gaining a stile in the field corner stay forward to the left of a fence to another stile, this time alongside a green metal five-barred gate. This permits access to a road by a T-junction at Rode Green. A signpost reads: "Marton 3, Gawsworth 2, Macclesfield 4 and Bosley 3."

Cross the junction directly to enter Pexhall Road with "Mile Corner Cottage" on your right. After 200 metres, and by a footpath finger post, turn left over a stile before walking along a broad track to the left of a hedge and, subsequently a fence. Over the stile by a five-barred gate stay with the track as it passes through a narrow belt of trees before curving slightly towards Manor Farm. One hundred metres before reaching the farm buildings, and where the track acquires a concrete surface, strike off to the right over the grass, aiming for an obvious stile by a five-barred gate alongside a small, cottage-like building.

On the far side of this stile continue forward and, staying to the right of the farm house, cross a cattle grid. Proceed down the farm drive-way. On meeting a Y-junction bear right so that North Rode church is directly ahead.

Pass through a galvanised five-barred gate with a cattle grid to reach a footpath sign a few yards before Lodge Cottage. Unless you wish to divert for a visit to the church, turn left by this sign to follow a track running between fences and passing yew Tree Farm on your right.

After 50 metres negotiate a waymarked stile and proceed directly ahead between two rows of large trees which, in April, are just bursting into leaf and which provide homes for a colony of grey squirrels which may be seen bobbing in and out of the holes in the trunks.

Lose altitude slightly to a stile which provides access to a broad track which, at one time or another, has enjoyed the benefits of a metalled surface. Turn right and, with a deciduous wood on the left and a hedge on the right, follow the track as it twists down the hill to a large lake which is blessed with kingfisher, mallard, coot and moorhen.

With the track climbing slightly, continue for about 500 metres until meeting a road on a ninety degree bend by Gateway Cottage. Stay forward over the railway bridge and pass the strangely shaped Beehive Cottage. Immediately before the bridge spanning the Macclesfield Canal turn left through a small white wooden gate onto the towpath.

With the canal on the right, stay on the towpath for approximately 3 kilometres. On the way pass the Bosley moorings, a mile stone indicating that Marple is 18 miles away and go under several bow-shaped bridges.

Continue well beyond Cowbrook Lane until reaching an elevated footbridge with a swing bridge with white railings, bridge number 49, just a few metres beyond. This carries the minor road from Gawsworth over the canal and is frequently opened at this time of year as pleasure boats pass on their way.

Close to the right-hand bank of the waterway is the A523, the main trunk road from Macclesfield to Leek and the Fool's Nook public house.

Pass beneath the footbridge and across the road to stay with the tow path for a further 500 metres, passing a SLOW sign and another mile post. Ten metres beyond this mile post, and 20 metres before a canal-side cottage, turn left by a small waymark to descend a short flight of steps to a wooden footbridge.

At the far end bear slightly left, climbing the field. Pass to the left of a large tree but to the right of some hawthorns as you make a direct line towards Woodhouse Green, the farm visible on the crest of the hill.

Negotiate a stile tucked-in close to the left-hand corner of an open barn and then turn right to pass on the outside of the farm complex before making a second turn to the right to a metal five-barred gate. Through that turn left along the farm driveway to meet the minor road linking Fool's Nook with Gawsworth. Turn right, passing Foden's Farm, crossing the railway bridge and then ignoring another

APRIL   GAWSWORTH

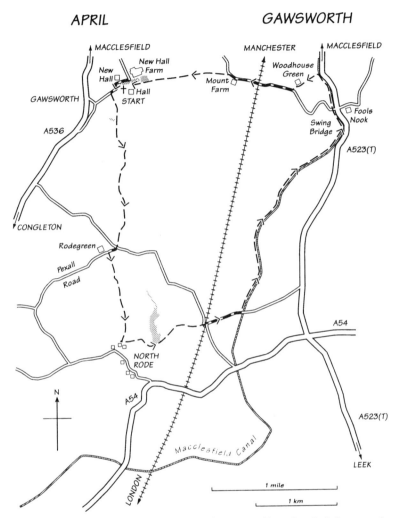

minor road, Crowbrook Lane, which goes off to the left by a red telephone kiosk.

Stay with the minor road until some 80 metres beyond Mount
Farm. Take a left turn onto an open grassy space and advance 20
metres to the footpath sign. Negotiate the adjacent kissing gate and
proceed up a slight slope to the right of a fence. Behind there is a fine
view of Shutlingsloe, Macclesfield Forest and the Pennines.

Maintain the same line of direction through another kissing gate, then a wicket gate before dropping down slightly to a waymarked stile. The fields hereabouts are large and, in April and May, resound to the song of the skylark and the calls of the lapwing, sounds which attract the kestrel which is often to be seen hovering overhead.

Beyond the stile the path widens into a track running between hedgerows before going through a metal five-barred gate to skirt to the left of the first of a series of lakes or fish ponds, noted for their marsh marigold and with Gawsworth New Hall beyond. Keep to the right of the Mews, known as Gawsworth Court, and to the left of the large statue of Sir Robert Peel.

On meeting the entrance drive to Gawsworth Hall turn right for a few metres to Church Lane. Turn left. The Hall, forming a splendid backdrop to the lake, is on your left. Follow the road as it passes the church, the Old Rectory and the New before turning sharply to the right for the final few metres back to the car.

May

Marbury

A walk through the rich pastoral landscape in the extreme south of the county visiting a fine viewpoint which offers a wonderful vista.

Route: Marbury Church – Big Mere – Wirswall Hill – Deemster Manor – Quoisley Hall – Steer Bridge – Shropshire Union Canal – Church Bridge – Little Mere – Marbury Church.

Terrain: Mainly field paths and tracks. One short moderate climb.

Start: Marbury Church. Map reference 561456.

Distance: 5 miles (8 kilometres).

Map: OS Explorer 257 - Crewe & Nantwich

Public Transport: Restricted bus service on certain weekdays and Saturdays from Whitchurch and Nantwich.

By Car: Leave the A41 at Bickley Moss, map reference 544480, and follow the minor road through Swanwick Green. There is limited parking on the church approach but please park with consideration for others.

Refreshments: The Swan Inn, Marbury, serves bar meals.

The Month

The name has come us through the Old French from the Latin *Maius*, meaning month of the goddess Maia. Traditionally, as far as England is concerned, May Day heralds the first day of summer, a feature which has been immortalised in the lines from the anonymous "Cuckoo Song" written about 1250:

"Summer is icumen in
Llude sing cuccu."

Until the Reformation the 1st May was one of the high days of the English calendar when customs originating in pagan times were adapted and perpetuated under the auspices of the Church. Colourful characters such as Jack-in-the-Green, Robin Hood, and Robin Goodfellow all formed an integral part of the rites and ceremonies while the ubiquitous maypole served as a focus for Morris Dancing, sports and other activities on the village green.

With the advance of Puritanism the celebrations declined until they were forbidden under Oliver Cromwell but revived with the Restoration of Charles II in 1660. A natural decline almost led to their total demise in the following century but a spate of Victorian revivals ensured that some, albeit a few, continued until the present day.

The most famous in Cheshire is the Royal Knutsford May Day Festival which dates from 1864. It contains all the traditional ingredients including the Rose Queen, Jack-in-the-Green, Morris Dancing and the maypole but it has also absorbed the more ancient and unique practice of "Sanding. This allegedly originated when King Canute of tidal fame forded the River Lily. On gaining the far bank he sat down to empty his boots of water. As he did so a wedding party was passing so the monarch wished the couple every happiness and as many children as there were grains of sand falling from his footwear.

So the custom developed of creating intricate patterns outside the houses of brides and grooms on their wedding days and now these same patterns are perpetuated by the town's official "Sander".

It was Shakespeare who commented on May weather when he wrote:

"Rough winds do shake the darling buds of May".

This apparently does bring certain benefits, at least according to another piece of ancient folk lore:

"A wet and windy May
Fills the barns with corn and hay."

Perhaps the most famous of all the proverbs associated with this month is one that still attracts considerable debate as to its exact meaning:

"Ne'er cast a clout till May is out."

Above all May is the month of blossom. The hedgerows are covered with the clustered flowers of the hawthorn, the hornbeam, the rowan and the apple. The horse chestnuts sport their numerous white candles of flowers. In the course of the month the countryside acquires more colour as such plants as the cuckoo flower, birdsfoot trefoil and those extensive swathes of bluebells bring a new dimension to the landscape. Roadside verges and country lanes are home to displays of cow parsley and hedge parsley as the umbellifers reach their peak.

These flowers, in turn, encourage the butterflies. May is the time to look for the orange-tips as they patrol the hedgerows in search of lady's smock and garlic mustard on which to lay their eggs. Meadow browns and whites are also often on the wing.

By May birdsong is at its peak with the arrival of the final summer migrants. Warblers, blackcaps, redstarts, pied flycatchers and the hirundines all add to the avian symphony created by blackbirds, thrushes, titmice, robins, willow warblers and others.

Many young mammals such as squirrels, voles, field mice, shrews and stoats make their first appearance and, if not seen, can be heard rustling through the under storey of the woodlands. For breeding birds it is also a hectic period as the parents work long hours to satisfy the rapacious appetites of their offspring and, by the close of the month, many of these may seen along the hedgerows.

Along the way

The Meres

At the close of the last Ice Age this area of South Cheshire was covered by a vast meltwater lake the last surviving remnants of which are the two meres at Marbury and those at Quoisley, Combermere and Blakemere. Overlooked by the church, the Big Mere helps to create an idyllic rural scene although the Little Mere is now virtually dried up and overgrown with vegetation.

Marbury

Marbury is one of the most attractive villages in the county containing many black and white cottages and houses so typical of this region of Cheshire. There is a red-brick house close to the church which boasts of beamed outer walls dating from at least 1550 along with various extensions added prior to 1700. The attractive village

green is noted for the large tree planted to commemorate
Wellington's victory at the Battle of Waterloo in 1815.

St Michael's Church

The parish church of St Michael which stands on an eminence
above the Big Mere is one of several in Cheshire with a fine perpendicular tower. More than 50 of these were constructed between 1400
and 1540 with teams of masons moving from parish to parish. Because of land subsidence, the tower has a lean of 25 inches from the
perpendicular and a Restoration Fund has been launched recently
in a move to correct the fault.

The church is believed to date from the fifteenth century although there are grounds for thinking that an ecclesiastical building
has occupied the site for more than 700 years. Inside are some
cast-iron grave slabs, perhaps made in the iron foundries of
Staffordshire and transported to Marbury by canal. Marbury boasts
the second oldest wooden pulpit in the county. It dates from 1456. If
any credence may be attached to local tradition then if the
1000-year-old yew tree in the churchyard falls it will be followed by

St Michael's Church

the collapse of the church. Today it is hollow but, because the inhabitants do not wish a catastrophe to happen, it is bound together with chains.

Shropshire Union Canal

Marbury stands on the Shropshire Union Canal which was formed through the amalgamation of several waterways. The main route of the waterway runs through Cheshire from Ellesmere Port to Audlem but there are several branches. Marbury is served by the Llangollen branch which links the Welsh town with the main part of the canal at Hurleston Junction, a short distance to the north-west of Nantwich.

Route Directions

Enter Marbury churchyard via the lych-gate and pass the western end of St Michael's Church before walking to the small wooden gate in the corner. Descend the field to the right of the Vicarage and then of a wall and fence to reach a stile. Do not negotiate this. Instead turn right walking along the lower boundary of the field with a hedge on your left. On reaching a small wooden gate, also on your left, turn right along the clear, well-trodden path as it heads across the meadow towards Big Mere which, as usual at this season of the year, is graced by swans.

By the corner of the mere negotiate stile before walking to the left of a wire fence and a bed of tall reed mace to a stile standing by a large metal gate. The next section of the route passes between a row of trees on the right, which effectively screens it from the mere, and a wood on the left. The path is lined with rosebay willowherb, horsetails, purple-headed thistles, nettles and brambles.

The path reaches another stile by a metal gate and, having emerged from the trees, continues forward along the boundary of a large meadow and to the right of a fence until reaching a stile with two waymarks. Ignore the route indicated by a South Cheshire Way symbol which bears left up Buttermilk Bank. Instead, opt to bear slightly to the right, gently ascending a shallow valley to an obvious waymarked stile on the far side of another large field.

Over this bear slightly leftwards and then right as the clear path climbs an arable field to another stile, this time by a small wooden gate. Beyond this there is a steep climb up an extensive undulating field. Initially stay to the right of three very large oak trees before bearing further right across open space while aiming for the right-hand end of a very tall hedge where it is joined by a metal fence. Negotiate the stile in this fence and turn left, climbing steeply to the right of the hedge, with a radio communication tower directly ahead. The next stile provides an exit onto the very narrow Wirswall Road close by Wickstead Hall which, although on your left, is effectively screened by trees.

At 142 metres above sea level this is the summit of Wirswall Hill which, on a clear day, offers a surprisingly extensive panorama as a reward for the effort of climbing. It embraces the Bickerton and Peckforton Hills, almost the whole of the Cheshire Plain, the Clwydian Hills in North Wales and even the Pennines. Marbury church is visible and, closer at hand, Quoisley Mere.

Over the stile, turn right along the road. After 10 metres, and by a footpath finger post, turn right over another stile so re-entering the field you have just left. This time, however, veer left down the slope, taking a bearing of the red brick Deemster Manor which lies at the base of the slope.

The path is somewhat vague but as it descends it passes a yellow waymark fixed to a redundant wooden gatepost which is immediately to the left of a clump of four hawthorn tree, obviously the relic of a hedgerow. Maintain direction, keeping to the right of the rotten stump of a tree and losing more altitude to another waymark, this time on the left-hand gatepost of a redundant gateway set into a hedge. Staying to the right of Deemster manor, veer left into the corner of the field where a stile with a finger post adjacent provides an exit onto a track. Turn left for a few metres to meet Wirswall Road opposite the Wirswall village sign.

Turn right along the road with Quoisley mere, screened by trees, on your left. The descent continues, albeit more gently, for a short distance before the road levels out. 50 metres beyond a metal five-barred gate on the left, and by two manhole covers sunk into the grass verge, veer left for about 5 metres to a wooden stile set deeply into the ledge. Continue to the right of a wire fence and where this

January: Mostyn House School, Parkgate

February: Macclesfield Forest

March: Swettenham church

June: Hankelow Hill

July: Siddington church

October: the bridleway to Bowstonegate

August: the approach to Three Shire Heads

November: Alderley Edge

MAY   MARBURY

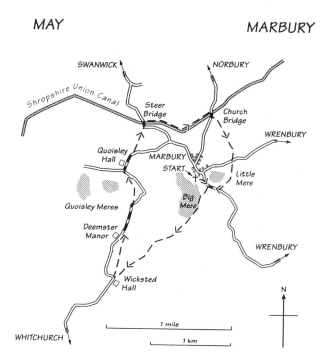

ends, swing right under some overhead wires to a stile in the far right-hand corner of a very long field.

Turn right over the stile which gives access to the road on an acute ninety degrees bend. Proceed along this road in the same direction, passing Quoisley hall on your left. Approximately 300 metres beyond turn left over a stile which has a footpath sign carrying the legend, "To Canal".

Bearing a few degrees to the left, head across the field to a stile by some hawthorns and then immediately cross a wooden footbridge before advancing just inside the boundary of Hadley Covert, the path running between two wire fences.

After 75 metres a waymarked stile is reached. Veer slightly to the right in crossing the next field while remaining some 5 metres to the left of a telegraph pole to meet another stile providing access to a road.

Turn left for the short distance to Steer Bridge which spans the

Shropshire Union Canal. Cross the bridge with its metal railings and, at the far end and opposite the Marbury village sign, make a left turn onto a short path leading to the canal tow path. Turn left along this to pass under Steer Bridge and stride out along the good turf path.

After approximately one kilometre Church Bridge is reached. Go through the small white wooden gate before turning right over Church Bridge, a metal affair spanning the Shropshire Union. Immediately afterwards cross a stone bridge and, almost at once and by a footpath sign, make a left turn over a stile.

Take a bearing diagonally right and cross a farm track to a conspicuous stile less than 100 metres distant and a little to the left of a telegraph pole. Maintain the same line of direction to the right of a row of large oak trees while climbing a very large field and aiming for another conspicuous though distant stile in the facing hedgerow. Over this waymarked stile bear right towards a hedge and, on reaching it, make a left turn, losing height to the corner of the field. Turn right over the stile there and remain to the right of a hedge until passing through a metal kissing gate to meet the road.

Again bearing slightly right, cross to a footpath sign and a metal kissing gate. Go forward with a hedge on your right in traversing the lower end of a large field which slopes upwards to your left. Negotiate another kissing gate and stay to the left of a fence for ten metres before passing the former mill that has been converted into a private house. From there, continue along the wide track, with the obscured Little Mere on your right, until passing through a kissing gate onto a narrow road.

Turn right for a few metres. Turn left through a small gate by the footpath sign and retrace your steps up the meadow to Marbury church.

June

Audlem

Starting from an ancient, historic village, this route traverses some of the most pretty scenery the county has to offer.

Route: Audlem – Mill Lane – Monk's Lane – the Parkes – Mill Plantation – Hankelow Mill – Monks Hall Farm – Bennett's Bridge – Moss Hall Aqueduct – Audlem.

Terrain: Mostly level with a minimum of undulation. Route follows several lanes, bridleways, field paths and canal tow path.

Start: Car park, Cheshire Road, Audlem. Map reference: 659437.

Distance: 5 miles (8 kilometres).

Map: OS Explorer 257 - Crewe & Nantwich

Public Transport: Audlem is served by a frequent daily bus service, including Sundays, from Crewe. There is a daily service (except Sunday) from Middlewich and Nantwich. Buses from Market Drayton on Wednesdays only and from Whitchurch and Hanley on Saturdays only.

By Car: Audlem may be reached by the A525 from Newcastle-under-Lyme and Whitchurch and the A529 from Nantwich and Market Drayton. There is a large car park off Cheshire Street close to the village centre.

Refreshments: Several pubs serve food while morning coffee, light lunches and afternoon teas are available at the Old Priest's House Coffee Shop and Tea Rooms in Vicarage Lane, directly opposite the church. (Open from 9.00 am to 5.00 pm or later every day, seven days a week all year.)

The Month

The name "June" has reached us by way of the old French from the Latin, "Junius", which means "Sacred to Juno", the Roman god. It is the month when the year reaches its central point, when the hours of daylight are at their maximum on June 21st and 22nd. The longest day is followed three days later by Midsummer Day, an apparent anomaly explained only by the fact that traditionally May 1st inaugurated the summer season. Because of the limited hours of darkness it is a favourite time of the year for overnight walks. Indeed, many rambling clubs feature such walks in their programmes.

Otherwise it is a month when we expect superb weather, hot and sunny with clear blue skies, a month for lazy strolls for many of us. For others, the prospect of long days on the hills encourages them to undertake long distance walks on the higher ground.

In the folklore calendar there are several major festivals, one of the most important being the feast of St Barnabas which is observed on the 11th June. Garlands of roses, lavender, rosemary and woodruff were worn and also used in the decoration of churches. Traditionally there is a Barnaby fair held in the Cheshire town of Macclesfield, although here they use the old, pre-Gregorian calendar with its ten-days difference. So now the celebration falls on the 22nd June. On the same date the inhabitants of Bunbury also staged their wake, a fair which involved events such as pony racing, wheelbarrow racing, archery, quoits, wresting and both bull and bear baiting.

Of even greater significance were Midsummer Night's Eve and Midsummer Day when the practice of lighting bonfires was once almost universal throughout the country. The origin of these is believed to date back to Druidical times. Another widespread custom was for young women to scatter hempseed in a meadow or in the churchyard at midnight in the hope of being able to conjure-up a vision of their future husband or lover. Midsummer Day was also a traditional date for village celebrations when churches were decorated and maypole dancing took place on the village green.

For those anxious about the weather prospects it should be remembered that:

> *"A dry May and a rainy June*
> *Puts the farmer's pipe in tune."*

On the other hand:

> *"A misty May and a hot June*
> *Makes the harvest come right soon."*

It is also worth remembering that:

> *"A swarm of bees in June is worth a silver spoon"*

One of the great delights of June is the profusion of flowers in the cottage gardens. They appear in every village as householders vie with each other to create the most colourful display. These are matched by the abundance of wild flowers in the countryside itself. Perhaps most noticeable are the meadows carpeted with buttercups and, quite often, poppies. The elder flowers add a touch of brilliant white to the hedgerows as though succeeding the May blossom of the previous month. These are rivalled by the pink flowers of the bramble and the dog rose.

Our lanes are flanked by displays of purple-headed thistles, foxgloves, ragged robin, birdsfoot trefoil, forget-me-nots, bugle, self-heal, honeysuckle, scabious, jack-by-the-hedge, tufted vetch, cuckoo pint and many other flowers. In some favoured habitats such as the abandoned lime beds at Plumley, near Northwich, there is a colourful abundance of wild orchids.

These vivid floral manifestations more than compensate for the noticeable decline in birdsong as the mating season draws to a close. Many birds, of course, are still to be seen flitting along or in-and-out of the hedgerows and trees. It is an excellent month for observing the swallows, swifts, house martins and sand martins.

June is the month when both the red and fallow deer give birth although, because they are usually hidden in the bracken, it is often difficult to see the calves. The back and sides of the red deer are originally dappled with white but these markings fade quickly and have vanished completely by the time the calf is two months old. Voles, wood mice, field mice and other small mammals are also with young but these are more often heard rustling about in the undergrowth than observed.

Along the way

Audlem

Audlem is recorded in the Domesday Book as Adelime, a name derived from a personal name, Alda, and lyme meaning a forest. Until comparatively recent times it played a pivotal role in the economy of South Cheshire. It not only provided a focus for local agriculture but was a vital centre of the cheese industry. Its importance was officially recognised in 1296 when King Edward 1 granted Thomas of

Adelyme a charter for the holding of a weekly market along with the privilege of an annual fair. The fair soon became obsolete but the market continued until the outbreak of the First World War.

A reminder of this is to be found in front of the parish church. It is the Buttercross. The present structure dates from 1733 and was used by local farmers for selling their cheese and butter. Alongside this is a large boulder with a ring in the centre which was once used for securing the bear owned by a man called Billy Boff and used for baiting.

The parish church, dedicated to St James the Great, was built in 1278 and given by Thomas de Adelyme to the Priory of St Thomas at Stafford. It was enlarged in the fourteenth century when the so-called "Weeping Chancel" was added. It was re-modelled in the sixteenth century and there have been more recent alterations following the discovery of death watch beetle and wet rot amongst the timbers.

One of the most alarming entries in the Parish Registers reads;

> "In September 1777 when the people were in church a great earthquake happened which shook the fabric so that a large stone fell out of one of the windows of the steeple."

The old Free Grammar School, founded in 1655, still stands. It served as a school until 1965 but is now a residential home for the elderly. Amongst the village's most famous natives was Geoffrey Whitney who published a celebrated "Book of Emblems" in 1586, a tome said to have been used by William Shakespeare.

Audlem gained a new lease of life with the building of the Shropshire Union Canal which opened in 1835. The 15 locks at Audlem carry the canal from the Shropshire heights to the Cheshire plain, a drop of 93 feet. Consequently there was an important wharf at Audlem, there being regular daily services between the village and Birmingham, London and Chester.

Every Saturday morning special cheese boats sailed to Manchester and other major towns. Eventually, however, the canal was superseded by the railway which arrived in 1863 and provided links with Nantwich, Market Drayton and Wellington from where there

On the Shropshire Union Canal , near Audlem

were connections to London and Shrewsbury. The axe of Dr. Beeching inevitably fell on the network in 1967.

Hankelow

The site of Hankelow Mill, which is passed during the walk, has been occupied by a mill for more than 300 years. According to local tradition there was a widow's curse on the building and in the nineteenth century there were three separate fires and on one occasion a wall collapsed. It is now a private residence.

Route Directions

Exit the car park by making a right turn into Cheshire Street but, after 100 metres and by the parish church and Buttercross, turn left along Staffordshire Street. Ignoring School Lane on the right continue beyond the Post Office and follow the road as it bends round tightly to meet the far end of School Lane.

There, turn left into a very narrow and unmarked road. After 100 metres and by Salford Lodge, a red brick house, turn left into Mill Lane which is signed as a public footpath. Immediately pass to the right of a bowling green and two bungalows. Hedged in now with hawthorn and bramble, and thick with meadow brown butterflies, the lane climbs gently until eventually it passes a large house on the right before levelling out to reach The Cottage which is on your left.

Beyond The Cottage the lane narrows into little more than a hedged path, flanked by clumps of ragwort, nettles and Himalayan Balsam. On warm summer days, the stillness is broken by the incessant buzz of bees and other insects.

After passing beneath a group of large deciduous trees and Mill House the lane reaches a footpath sign at its junction with Monks Lane, now a narrow metalled road but once used by the monks of Combermere Abbey on their journeys to Audlem.

Turn left for approximately 200 metres but, by a footpath sign, turn right into the approach to The Parkes. On nearing this prestigious house, and where the white railings commence, turn left for ten metres over the grass and then make a right turn over the partially obscured stile in the field corner.

Advance along the same line of direction while remaining close to the hedge on the left, following the boundary of a very large field until reaching a footpath sign by a white metal kissing gate which allows an exit onto the A529, the Audlem to Nantwich road.

Turn left. Ignore the first stile on the right which is set deeply into the hedge. Stay with the main road, passing the Hankelow village sign. Just prior to another sign, this time warning of elderly people, and by another footpath post, turn right into another Mill Lane, this time leading to Hankelow Mill.

Initially it is flanked by hedges on the top of banks but then passes through Mill Plantation, a mixture of deciduous trees with a scattering of Scots Pines. There is a lush under storey of nettles, ferns, ivy, brambles and red campion with a narrow stream flowing on your left.

After several hundred metres the lanes passes to the left of The Mews before bending round to pass to the left of the mill which closed in 1972 and is now a private residence with a most colourful garden, the floral decor being completed by hanging baskets and window boxes.

Continue over the bridge spanning the infant River Weaver with

JUNE   AUDLEM

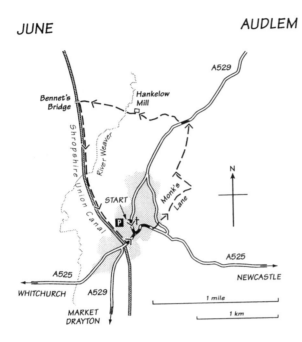

its mallard and banks of poppies before crossing a cattle grid for a
short climb followed by a level stretch. Where Mill Lane bends
round to the right towards Banks Hall Farm, maintain the original
direction across ten metres of greensward to a waymarked post and
wooden stile.

Over that, veer diagonally right across the field to another stile
adjacent to a five-barred gate in the corner. This stile provides access
to a lane running from right to left. Cross this and advance up a facing lane which is initially fenced but then hedged. After some 200
metres climb slightly towards Bennett's Bridge but do not cross it.
rather, turn right through a small metal gate located adjacent to the
start of the brick parapet. Descend the short path to the tow path of
the Shropshire Union Canal. Turn left, pass under the bridge and
proceed in the direction of Audlem with the canal on your right.

In due course the tow path crosses the aqueduct spanning the
River Weaver before continuing to Moss Hall bridge with its attendant pair of mute swans. Moss Hall is to your left.

This bridge marks the beginning of the Audlem series of locks.

Climb by the first of these to a mile post which reads, "Nantwich 6 miles, Autherley junction 33 miles and Norbury Junction 17½ miles."

Continue alongside the locks, pass to the right of "The Shroppie Fly", a canalside pub, and then veer left onto a broad, surfaced lane which soon meets Shropshire Street by the Bridge Inn. Turn left and, at the road junction by the church and Buttercross, make another left turn into Cheshire Street for the return to the car park.

July

Redesmere

A gentle stroll which embraces lakeside and parkland in central Cheshire.

Route: Redesmere — Fanshawe Lane — A34 — Capesthorne Hall — Mill Lane — Park Farm — Siddington — Redesmere.

Terrain: A level route along field paths, tracks and bridleway.

Start: Parking area on Fanshawe Lane, Siddington, facing Redesmere. Map reference 848714. Because of the nature of this parking facility, extreme caution is urged when both driving and walking, especially if you have children.

Distance: 3 miles (4.8 kilometres)

Map: OS Explorer 268 - Macclesfield & Congleton

Public Transport: None.

By Car: Redesmere is reached by a minor road off the A34, approximately midway between Alderley Edge and Congleton. If approaching from the north, turn left a very short distance beyond Siddington Village Hall. If approaching from the south turn right a short distance after the junction of the A34 with the B5392, Macclesfield to Holmes Chapel road.

Refreshments: Tea Rooms at Capesthorne Hall during opening hours. Otherwise a refreshment van selling ice cream and snacks at week-ends and busy periods in the parking area at Redesmere.

The Month

The seventh month of the year takes its name from Julius Caesar. Almost imperceptibly the days begin to shorten, although it remains one of the busiest holiday months of the year.

Apart from St Swithin's Day, there are few notable folklore customs during this month, and most of these are really of little more than local interest. The 15th July is said to be the arbiter of our weather for the following forty days, as the ancient saw reminds us:

> *"St Swithin's Day, if thou dost rain,*
> *For forty days it will remain:*
> *St Swithin's Day, if thou be fair,*
> *For forty days, 'twill rain nae mair."*

This tradition arose because when the bones of the saint were transferred to the new Cathedral at Winchester in 971 it rained or, as an ancient chronicle put it, "The saint protested and wept". Unfortunately there is no evidence that it did rain for the subsequent forty days.

It is also a quiet spell for bird life. The glorious birdsong of the mating season has faded and, apart from the disappearance of the cuckoo, there is little in the way of avian migration, either into this country or away from it. The principal exception being the adult shelduck which migrate to the Heligoland Bight off the German coast where they congregate for moulting, leaving this year's offspring in creches guarded by non-breeding birds.

There is still a profusion of wild flowers to be seen, both in the meadows and in the hedgerows which, with their recent growth are assuming a more unkempt appearance. The verges and hedge bottoms are filled with luxuriant growths of nettles. Dock leaves are common and, near many meres and water courses the rhubarb-like leaves of the butterbur, which flowered in February, grow in profusion. Violet, self-heal, foxglove, blue scabious, yellow ragwort and skullcap with its tiny blue flowers all add to the variety of floral delights to be found on most walks. The grasses, nettles and many of the wild flowers are growing to enormous heights, especially the giant hogweeds. On the uplands of East Cheshire the bog cotton or cotton grass provides a pleasing splash of white to the sombre moorlands while lush bilberries are usually ripe for picking – if you have the patience.

Insects of all types, but especially butterflies, dragonflies and hover flies, are common and under certain weather conditions the midges may become something of a nuisance.

Along the way

Redesmere

Redesmere is a popular spot with picnickers from Macclesfield, Congleton and other local towns and is noted for its abundant water birds including mallard, swans, Canada Geese, coot, moorhen, heron and occasional rarer visitor. One of the most unusual features of the lake is a floating island which, to stop its straying, is now anchored to the eastern edge.

Redesmere

Capesthorne Hall

Capesthorne has been occupied by the Bromley Davenport family for almost a millennium because the ancestors of the present owners were recorded as occupying the site in the Domesday Book of 1086. The hall itself has undergone several reconstructions, the present one dating from the eighteenth century. The interior boasts several impressive features including the Bromley Staircase with its family portraits, the American Room furnished in the New World style, the Drawing Room, noted for its double fireplace, and the State Dining Room.

The landscaped parkland features a string of lakes which are approached through a set of Milanese gates. The gateposts of the courtyard carry stone carvings of a felon's head, a reminder of the days were in charge of the Forest of Macclesfield and their word was law.

Siddington

All Saints' Church, Siddington, is more than seven centuries old, the earliest recorded mention dating from 1337 although it was not licensed for preaching until 1521. The weight of its Kerridge stone roof proved too great for its timber frame, filled-in with wattle and daub, and, in the nineteenth century, the walls started to bulge. To prevent their utter collapse they were strengthened by building outer walls of local brick, some of which were painted in black and white to resemble the original timbers which are still standing.

The fourteenth century rood screen was originally painted and gilded while the pulpit was part of a three-decker. In the Chancel wall there is a small hole which may once have been a leper's squint through which those afflicted by the disease could observe the service while remaining isolated from the remainder of the congregation.

The "Cock Loft" above the west end has been a nesting site of a jackdaw for many years and when the straw was removed recently it filled twenty sacks. Outside, beneath a large oak tree, are the gravestones of several members of the Bromley-Davenport family. The churchyard also contains the graves of two Canadian airmen who crashed nearby during the Second World War. The giant yew tree is claimed to be as old as the church itself which is locally renowned for its annual service of blessing the animals, held on the first Sunday of June.

Route Directions

Facing Redesmere and with your back to the parking area, turn right along Fanshawe Lane so walking away from the A34. The lake is on the left and gently rolling pastureland to the right. 100 metres beyond the far corner of the lake, and with a Peak and Northern Footpath Society sign indicating a footpath to Capesthorne, turn left over a wooden stile.

Walking the well-trodden path, stay along the left-hand boundary of the meadow with deciduous trees, mainly oak, on your left and Fanshawe Farm a short distance away to the right. In July this is an excellent area to see dragonflies and meadow brown butterflies.

In the far corner of the field negotiate another waymarked stile before proceeding along the path as it makes its way between trees on the left and a wire fence on the right to another wooden stile. There is a brick cottage with a thatched roof nearby on the right. Stay forward between two wire fences, cross a wooden footbridge after 100 metres and, after a further 40 metres, bear left to a five-barred gate with a bridleway sign alongside.

Continue straight ahead to the left of the Redesmere Sailing Club until meeting a wide track. Bear right along this, keeping to the right of the lake. After approximately 500 metres, and some 50 metres before a wooden five-barred gate, is a footpath sign. Turn left by this, cross the grass for 15 metres and then traverse a small concrete footbridge which leads to a small wood by the edge of the lake.

After a further 100 metres, and by a chestnut paling fence, bear slightly right for 5 metres and turn left over a wooden footbridge. Stay to the immediate right of the chestnut fencing to a gap in the facing hedge with a footpath sign adjacent. This provides an exit onto the busy A34 with an old-fashioned milestone which reads, "Congleton 6¾: Alderley Edge 4 and Wilmslow 6"

Taking great care, cross directly to the opposite pavement and then turn right, walking about eight metres to another footpath sign. Turn left over the stile to use the clear, well-defined path along the right-hand field boundary. In the first corner there is a small lake with an old boat house on the far bank. In July its surface is covered with the broad leaves and yellow flowers of the water lily.

By this lake turn sharp left to a wooden, waymarked stile within 50 metres. Having negotiated this make a right turn through ninety degrees to walk to the left of a wire fence. Where this corners away leftwards, continue directly ahead across the meadowland with another, somewhat longer lake now on your right.

Soon Capesthorne Hall itself comes into view on the far side of the lake while you reach a black, metal kissing gate which stands by the end of an ornamental red brick bridge. Note that there is no access onto this bridge which is guarded by a five-barred gate.

Through the kissing gate, ignore the 45 degree left turn indicated by the arm of the footpath finger post, opting instead to maintain the general line of direction a little to the left of the lake. Where this terminates, stay forward to a wooden stile by a double five-barred gate with another footpath sign. Proceed along the subsequent wide track with a group of Scots Pines on your immediate right until passing to the left of a small bungalow to meet Mill Lane.

Cross this narrow, surfaced road more or less directly to a stile with a sign indicating a route to Siddington. Although the path is not clear on the ground, leave a small pond on your right to strike out over the field diagonally left, taking aim for the next stile which is clearly visible. Maintain the same line of direction to a second stile before veering slightly right to cross a wide farm track to a stile by a telegraph pole.

Pass a circular metal water trough before remaining to the immediate right of a wire fence for 20 metres to a waymarked stile followed by a planked footbridge. At the far end turn left, as waymarked, and continue to the left of another hedge. Where this corners left after 100 metres follow it round, passing under overhead wires to a waymarked stile after a further 50 metres.

Cross another planked footbridge and stay forward with a hedge on your left and trees on your right. until meeting a waymarked stile after 100 metres. Over this continue forward a short distance along the perimeter of the yard of Park Farm until your route is barred by a large pair of tubular galvanised steel gates displaying a notice, "No public right of way".

Do not despair. Rather, bear right along the wide track between the farm buildings, staying with it as it corners left to pass through two more metal five-barred gates. Walk to the right of the house of Park Farm to regain Mill Lane.

Turn right for approximately 400 metres. On reaching a footpath sign alongside a five-barred gate, turn right over a wooden stile taking direction from the arm of the finger post. Once again the path is far from distinct so remain immediately to the right of two large trees, aiming towards a wood on the left.

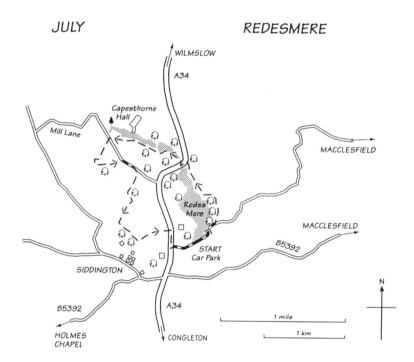

JULY   REDESMERE

Negotiate a stile in a barbed wire fence, advance a few metres to a second and then stay to the right of a wood for about 20 metres. There, corner left to another stile by a five-barred gate with a foot-path sign. There is a cottage nearby on the left.

Negotiate the stile to stay to the left of a hedge while climbing for 100 metres with Jodrell Bank Radio Telescope hoving into view in the far distance. The gradient levels before losing height to a field corner where a stile permits an exit onto a very narrow, hedged bridleway with a white, thatched cottage a few yards to the right.

Turn left along this bridleway where the rampant verges are lush with rosebay willowherb, hogweed, hedge parsley, lucerne and holly. Soon the hedge on the right is replaced by woodland and the ground falls steeply away to a stream.

On reaching a T-junction after several hundred metres make a left turn into another bridleway which leads to a junction by a cottage and a wooden garage after 50 metres. Turn right onto the wider track, passing between a couple of ponds before eventually meeting the A34.

Turn right and, using the pavement along this busy road, head southwards for 200 metres before turning left into Fanshawe Lane. After 75 metres turn left through a small wooden gate to enter the picnic area and then turn sharply right. Head for the far end of the picnic area to follow the path which runs to the left of a hedge for 100 metres before emerging by the lake and parking area.

August

The Cat and Fiddle

A strenuous but rewarding upland walk across moorlands carpeted in purple heather which provides some of the finest views in England.

Route: Cat and Fiddle – Cumberland Brook – Cumberland Clough – Sparbent – Holt Farm – Three Shire Heads – Blackclough – Reeve Edge – Danebower Hollow – Cat and Fiddle.

Terrain: Bridleways and moorland paths with several steep climbs. May be muddy after rain.

Start: Cat and Fiddle Inn on the A537 Macclesfield to Buxton road. map reference 001719

Distance: 6½ miles (10 kilometres)

Map: "The Peak District: White Peak Area". No. 24 in the OS Outdoor Leisure series.

Public Transport: A new service in conjunction with Virgin Rail provides several buses daily, including Sundays, between Macclesfield, the Cat and Fiddle, Buxton and Bakewell.

By Car: The Cat and Fiddle is located about midway between Macclesfield and Buxton on the A537. There is parking opposite the Cat and Fiddle.

Refreshments: The Cat and Fiddle serves meals at lunch time and in the evening.

The Month

The eighth month of the year takes its name from Augustus Caesar, the first Roman Emperor. For us in the 21st century it is traditionally associated with high summer and, because of the pattern of the school year, is the height of the holiday season. However, in medieval England it heralded the arrival of Autumn. Lammas Eve, the 1st August, signalled the date of the transition from Summer. Lammas, originally "Loaf Mass", was formerly a significant church holiday or Holy Day, and traditionally loaves of bread were baked from the first fruits of the harvest. As with so many festivals, it was adapted from a previous pagan festival by the early church and Christianised. When England was still mainly an agrarian society, August was always regarded as a harvesting month and so very much a part of the Autumn scene.

Another important feast day during the month was St Bartholomew's Day, the 24th, when numerous local fairs were held including the most famous of them all at Smithfield in London. The weather wise would tell you that:

"If St Bartholomew's be fine and clear
You may hope for a prosperous Autumn that year."

Nowadays one of the most famous dates is the 12th August, the start of the grouse shooting season. It is thanks to this sport that many stretches of moorland remain covered with heather which flowers this month and provides our uplands with that glorious purple cloak. If it were not for the management of the moors for shooting, more of them would have disappeared to provide sheep grazing.

The hedgerows are still full of flowers, although many are past their best. August is the month when the air is filled with 'Angels', the seed heads of thistles removed by even the gentlest of breezes. The first of the blackberries will have ripened so that the keen-eyed walker will have an excuse for loitering to taste one of the most delightful of fruits and perhaps even collect a few to take home for inclusion in an apple pie. The rowans are sporting their clusters of red berries in preparation for the arrival of the winter birds.

No rural scene in August would be complete without a village cricket match and, for those out and about on Saturday and Sunday afternoons, this is yet another excuse to linger, so enjoying the late summer sunshine as the days begin to shorten.

Along the way

This high-level route crosses the roof of England, traversing wild moorlands before descending towards Wildboarclough and then climbing up to the A54 and descending again towards and alongside the infant River Dane. It passes briefly into the neighbouring county of Derbyshire as it climbs away from Three Shire heads and follows field paths towards and then through the now-defunct Reeve Edge quarries. It climbs by an ancient chimney to follow a former pack-horse route towards the Cat and Fiddle. The upland stretches of this walk command panoramic views of the finest moors in the Peak District National Park including Kinder Scout, Shining Tor, the Roaches, Hen Cloud, Croker Hill and Shutlingsloe, the so-called Matterhorn of Cheshire because of its distinctive summit. On clear days the vista ranges across the whole of the Cheshire Plain to embrace the Clwydian Hills in North Wales and much of North Staffordshire.

Cat and Fiddle

Standing at 1,690 feet (519 metres) above sea level, the Cat and Fiddle is the second highest licensed public house in England, being but a few feet lower than Tan Hill in North Yorkshire. It occupies a lonely location on the A537 roughly mid way between Buxton and Macclesfield, and it is often cut off by winter snows. It was built by John Ryle, a Macclesfield banker, to cater for the needs of travellers using the newly turnpiked road. The date of its construction is uncertain but one visitor, writing in 1831, described it as "newly erected". Its name is variously ascribed as either a corruption of Catherine Fidelis, a reference to Catherine of Aragon, the first wife of Henry VIII, or to the nursery rhyme, "Hey diddle diddle, the cat and the fiddle".

Three Shire Heads

Three Shire Heads is the point where the boundaries (or heads) of Cheshire, Derbyshire and Staffordshire meet; the name is not Three Shires Head because, of course, there are three 'heads'. On John Speed's map of 1610 it was marked as Three Shires Stones, one for each county, but traces of these have long since disappeared. It is believed that the present packhorse bridge was already in existence at that date. Panniers Pool, just below the bridge, may have been the original fording point, although it is claimed that the Jaggers or packhorse men used it for watering their horses, hence its name.

The bridge, which spans the River Dane, was the meeting place of four packhorse routes. At some point in its history it was widened,

The bridge and pool at Three Shire Heads

either because of the volume of traffic or to permit the passage of carts. Today it is not accessible to vehicles of any kind and is the preserve of the walker and horse rider.

One of the old routes climbs out of the valley by Cut-Thorn Hill before descending into Wildboarclough and then out across the Cheshire Plain to the salt towns of the county – Nantwich, Middlewich and Northwich. This was one of the popular routes for transporting salt across the Pennines into Lincolnshire and other eastern counties. Another route climbs from Three Shire Heads to the Derbyshire village of Flash before striking out for Buxton or into Hollinsclough and southwards towards Hartington. The one on the Staffordshire bank of the River Dane heads for Gradbach, where there was once a thriving mill, before continuing across the hills to Wildboarclough or further down the Dane valley towards Congleton and the salt towns. The fourth route climbs to Danebower Hollow before crossing the moors to the Cat and Fiddle and thence into the Goyt Valley northwards or, again, turning towards Buxton.

Route Directions

From the Cat and Fiddle cross the A537 onto the signed bridleway opposite which, initially, runs almost due south across open moorlands with extensive views in almost every direction. In recent years, this track had been upgraded and, after approximately 500 metres, a small new bridge carries it over what was formerly a very deep peat trough. Beyond the bridge the gradient increases almost imperceptibly as the track makes its way through a mixture of heather, white cotton grass and bilberry.

Eventually, as the top of the gradient is reached, there is a clear but distant view of the Roaches and Hen Cloud in the Staffordshire Moorlands near Leek. After approximately one kilometre the bridleway bends slightly left before passing between two redundant gateposts lacking their gate and then picking up a row of fencing posts, without any wire, on the left. To the right there is an absorbing view of Shutlingsloe.

Approximately 500 metres further on the track reaches one of the old-fashioned Peak and Northern Footpath Society signs indicating a path to Wildboarclough by way of Cumberland Clough. Turn right onto this, following a clear path as it wends it way gradually down the grass slope. Soon, however, the rate of descent quickens. On gaining a derelict stone wall keep it on your left until a sudden sharp drop of about 20 metres leads to the right-hand bank of Cumberland Brook.

As the path moves further down the clough it widens before finally forming a T-Junction with a wide bridleway coming up the valley from Wildboarclough. The junction has a three-armed finger post. Turn left along this bridleway, soon climbing steeply to the left of Wood Moss. When the gradient finally levels-out, the track passes the derelict remains of Sparbent Farm, which are on the right, before losing height slightly and passing through a wooden five-barred gate to the A54, the Buxton to Congleton road.

Cross directly to a footpath sign. Negotiate the newly-installed crash barrier before descending a flight of seven wooden steps and bearing ever so slightly to the left in crossing the field to a stone step stile. Continue down the subsequent sloping field to the right-hand corner and turn right through a gate. Immediately turn left as indicated by a white arrow on a gatepost.

Remain close to the wall on your left and, in the following field corner, bear right, passing two five-barred gates in quick succession on your left. Both are waymarked and both the bear the legend, "Private". Soon the wall is replaced by a wire fence and the River Dane appears as little more than a stream down below.

The excellent grass path makes for good walking as you lose height to a wooden five-barred gate. Pass through this and immediately ignore a stile on your left. Maintain the general line of direction along the stony track, passing over a culverted stream coming in from the right. The bridleway descends the narrowing valley which has rounded sloping moorlands on either side.

In August the air is thick with the floating seed heads of the numerous thistles and the slopes are dressed with bracken, heather and bilberry with the occasional stunted oak. Apart from the continuous sound of running water there is absolute silence: the area has the feeling of wilderness and remoteness. Occasionally there is the sight of a heron rising from the banks of the infant Dane or of a kestrel hovering.

On reaching the waymarker post at Three Shire Heads turn left to cross the ancient packhorse bridge which, incidentally, makes an excellent spot for a coffee break. At the far end of the bridge do not turn right but continue ahead through a five-barred metal gate to embark on another climb along another bridleway, this time in Derbyshire. It runs through Black Clough.

At the first junction fork left into a shallow valley and negotiate another metal five-barred gate across the entrance of the driveway leading to Black Clough House. Turn left over the cattle grid for a steepish climb of some 200 metres. Where the driveway bends, turn left through another five-barred gate, pass in front of the farm house and exit the premises through a third five-barred gate.

Continue directly ahead to the right of a drystone wall, the path soon widening as it passes through a wall gap and remains alongside the wall. Where this wall corners away to the left, veer right across the field to a gateway. Through this turn sharply to the left onto a widening path which runs along the contour with a wall on the left.

AUGUST   THREE SHIRE HEADS

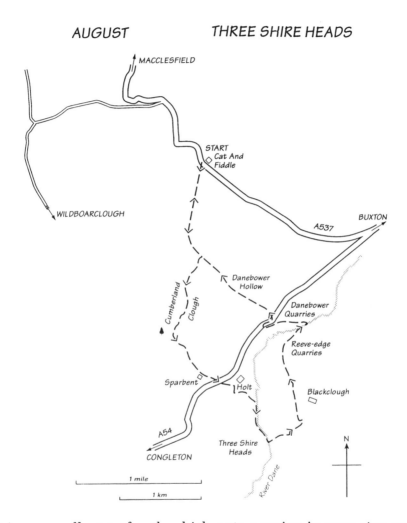

It is an excellent turf path which puts a spring in your step and makes for some great walking.

After a considerable distance it arrives at the abandoned workings of Reeve Edge Quarries and widens into a track. Where this curves round to the right stay forward, keeping your original line of direction, though now along a narrower path indicated by a small post with a yellow waymark.

Pass the spoil heaps and derelict buildings before the path widens again into a broad track and descends to the banks of the River Dane, at this point no more than a stream. On reaching the river turn left, as indicated by another yellow waymark, cross by the stepping stones and, on the far side, veer slightly right to climb a small bank.

By the next waymark turn left for 20 metres before ascending a short stretch of scree. At the top stay forward along the track which formerly served the Danebower Quarries. This track climbs gradually towards a prominent stone chimney, a relic of a coal mine which once occupied the site.

By this chimney pass through a wooden five-barred gate and, at once, make a sharp right turn onto a narrow path which ascends steeply to a footpath finger post and the A54. Negotiate the metal crash barrier and, exercising extreme caution, cross the road bearing slightly right to the facing bridleway sign. Here there are no stiles or other barriers to impede access onto another refurbished track which slowly climbs onto the high moors between Whetstone Ridge on the right and Danebower on the left, providing panoramic views of this region of the Peak District National Park.

Continue along this bridleway for more than 2.5 kilometres of level walking across the moors to reach the A537, emerging opposite the Cat and Fiddle.

September

Farndon

A peaceful, tranquil riverside walk along the international border where violence once reigned.

Route: Farndon — Townfield Lane — Knowl Lane — Churton — Marsh Lane — Starlings Wood — Farndon.

Terrain: Mainly field paths and bridleways with one long stretch alongside the River Dee. May be muddy, especially after wet weather. No steep ascents.

Start: Car park near the church, Farndon. Map reference 413545

Distance: 5½ miles (9 kilometres).

Map: OS Explorer 257 - Crewe & Nantwich

Public Transport: There is a frequent daily (including Sundays) bus service linking Farndon with both Wrexham and Chester.

By Car: Farndon is signed from the A534 Wrexham to Nantwich road at map reference 421540. It may also be approached directly from Chester by the B5130. The car park near the church is signed from the centre of the village. There is also a small car park by the medieval bridge.

Refreshments: Several pubs in Farndon and the White Horse at Churton serve meals at lunch time and during the evenings.

The Month

Although it is the ninth month of the year, September takes its name from *Septem*, the seventh month of the Roman year which commenced in March. It also marks the season of 'mists and mellow fruitfulness' because it is the month of the harvest. Evidence for this is to be found in the many harvest festivals held in villages and churches throughout the land and, on the trees and plants of the countryside where there is an abundance of berries and fruits. Many of the berries will provide sustenance for the overwintering birds whose numbers will be swollen by flocks of immigrants from Scandinavia and the Continent as they start to arrive at the close of the month.

In the hedgerows many of the wild flowers will have died, only their brown withering stems to remind us of their summer glory. During September many of the leaves on the deciduous trees will begin to transform their colour, becoming yellow, brown and even vermilion.

Early in the month flocks of swallows will gather on telegraph wires and other perches in preparation for their long flights to Africa and other summer visitors will also be departing. On the coast, in particular the Dee Estuary, the first of the winter waders will start to arrive. It is a month of dramatic change, a signal that summer is over and winter on its way. Gradually the temperatures will fall and the first of the frosts may be experienced. However, September often produces an Indian Summer when temperatures are high and the skies blue and sunny, ideal for walking.

Butterflies, especially red admirals, tortoiseshells and peacocks will still be plentiful during the early days and the small mammals will remain active in the under storey. It is also a good month for the harvest mouse. The vole and the wood mouse emerge to collect nuts for their winter stores as do the grey squirrels. This is the month when the ferns are at their most conspicuous because the increasing dampness of the hedgerow suits them. In the damp mornings, the webs of the spiders glisten in the sunshine, the most common being those of the garden or orb spider. In the fields and woodlands mushrooms and other fungi appear, now at their best.

Perhaps the most celebrated of September's feasts was that of St Michael on the 29th. It was a traditional date for the payment of rents and the settling of accounts. In many towns and villages fairs were held and it was customary to eat goose, then considered to be at its best because it had been fattened on the stubble left in the fields after the harvest had been garnered.

For any wishing to ponder the forthcoming weather prospects it should be noted that "a south wind on the 20th, 21st or 22nd may foretell three months of warm weather, but should they be wet, stormy days then the ensuing winter will be sunless."

Along the way

Farndon

During the medieval period Farndon, because of its position on the bank of the River Dee, always played a prominent role in Anglo-Welsh affairs. It was frequently the scene of conflict and often suffered from border raids as the Welsh descended on the fertile Cheshire Plain in search of cattle and other plunder. It was at Farndon that the two sons of the Welsh prince, Madoc, were drowned in the river by their guardians who planned to succeed to their inheritance. Even to this day their ghosts are reputed to haunt the district and there are some who will swear to having heard their screams.

These were not the only royal deaths associated with this border village. In 924 King Edward the Elder died there of natural causes and his body was afterwards taken to Winchester for burial.

In Anglo-Saxon times it was known as Ferentone, meaning 'fern-covered hill' and by the Domesday Book of 1086 this had evolved into Ferendon. It lies on the route of an old Roman road so it is likely that either a ford or a ferry existed there from the earliest days.

Its significance was enhanced in 1345 when the monks of St Werburgh's Abbey, Chester, constructed the fine medieval bridge which still spans the river, so linking England and Wales. By then, the conflict between the two countries was virtually at an end and Cheshire was enjoying a period of economic growth. The bridge facilitated the transport of salt and other goods across into the Principality. The fine red sandstone structure is now listed as an ancient monument.

In the seventh century St Chad, Bishop of Lichfield in which the diocese of Farndon was then located, visited the area and so the church was dedicated to him. A church bearing this dedication is known to have existed there long before the Norman Conquest and it was probably re-built or re-constructed at some point during the economic boom of the fourteenth and fifteenth centuries. Part of the original building was destroyed by fire in the 1600s, which resulted in it being described in 1622 as 'a fair new building'

The medieval bridge at Farndon

During the Civil War it was occupied by the Parliamentarian forces and suffered extensive damage that resulted in another reconstruction in 1658 when clerestories and arcades were added and the tower heightened. The events of these turbulent years are recorded in a stained glass window to be found in the Barnston Chapel. This shows several local gentry who upheld the Royalist cause including Sir Francis Gamul, Sir Richard Grosvenor and Sir William Mainwaring. In the church there is also a memorial to Roger Barnston who fought during the Crimean War and died during the Indian Mutiny. There is also a very conspicuous obelisk to his memory on the outskirts of the village along the Chester road.

Another famous native was John Speed, the celebrated Elizabethan cartographer, who lived from 1552 to 1629. He was responsible for producing the first maps of the English counties.

Farndon used to be renowned for its strawberries and, until overtaken by the Roodee at Chester, had the most prominent racecourse in Cheshire. The races were held on the Hay and often watched by spectators on the Welsh bank of the river.

Churton

Although it no longer exists, a stone cross formerly stood at the main cross roads in Churton. Hob and Pump Lane, both included in this walk, divided the village into two parishes, Churton-by-Aldford and Churton-by-Farndon, but, despite its name, the village never had a church of its own.

There are several distinctive buildings in Churton including Churton Hall Farm which is a Grade 2 listed Elizabethan manor house, several seventeenth century black and white cottages and two rows of Victorian villas. Quarry Cottage, once a coaching inn which still retains its black-leaded grate, has been in the same family for two centuries. At Almere on the River Dee there used to be a flat-bottomed punt which was employed as a ferry.

Route Directions

Leave the car park opposite Farndon church by turning right and, after a mere 20 metres, turning right again, this time into Church Street. After approximately 75 metres this meets the High Street, or main road through the village. Cross to the facing pavement and make a left turn. By the Post Office turn right into Churton Road.

Walk along Churton Road for a short distance but, by the far boundary of the Junior School, turn right into what appears to be the drive to a private house. There is no footpath sign at this point. After 60 metres, and by the actual entrance to the house driveway, veer right along a narrow fenced path which goes behind the school and then the playing field to a metal kissing gate. Turn right and stay to the left of a hedge with Raw Head, Bickerton Hill and the Peckforton Hills all clearly visible in the far distance ahead.

Pass through a second metal kissing gate, this time waymarked, and advance for 5 metres to another on your right. Do not use this. Rather make a left turn along another path which runs some 20metres to the right of a hedge as it traverses a narrow field.

By a footpath finger post at the corner of another hedge, this time on your right, turn right and walk with a very tall hedge on your left. Where this hedge corners away to the left, maintain direction over an open field for approximately 100 metres to another footpath sign and a stile adjacent to a metal five-barred gate. This grants an exit onto the B5130.

Turn left for 100 metres and, by a footpath post reading "Churton 3.5 kilometres and Coddington 3.5 kilometres, make a right turn through a double wooden five-barred gate onto a surfaced track. Stay to the left of some farm buildings and remain with this concrete track, negotiating a somewhat ramshackle double five-barred gate on the way. Eventually the surface terminates in a gateless gateway with a waymarker sign on the adjacent fence. Bear diagonally left across the next field to cross a small planked footbridge and a stile immediately beyond in the left-hand field corner.

Advance to the right of a fence and hedge which at this time of year is full of ripe luscious blackberries to a small wooden gate followed by a wooden footbridge and a wooden footpath finger post reading, "Crewe 2.8 kilometres, Farndon 2 kilometres and Churton 2.3 kilometres."

Turn left along Marsh Lane, a bridleway which at this stage forms a section of the Bishop Bennet way, a long distance route for horse riders covering 34 miles of bridleways and byways in south-west Cheshire. It runs from Beeston Castle to Wirswall, near Whitchurch, by way of Tattenhall, Churton and Malpas and it is hoped that soon it may be extended through Shropshire to Shrewsbury.

Marsh Lane is wide and grassy. After 200 metres a footpath sign is reached indicating a route to Coddington striking off to the right. Ignore this. Rather stay forward along Marsh Lane by negotiating a wooden, waymarked five-barred gate. The lane is hedged. The hawthorns are a brilliant red with their haws, the oaks are laden with fresh green acorns, the roses are laden with hips, while the verges are full of dried brown stems of grass waving gently in the breeze and the umbellifers are topped with dead seed heads. There are even a few shrivelled-up elderberries still clinging to the branches. In September there are birds still flitting in and out of the trees while butterflies, including tortoiseshells, are on the wing as are the dragonflies.

Several small ponds are scattered across the adjacent fields, perhaps a relic of the marsh which once existed and which gave its name to the lane.

SEPTEMBER   FARNDON

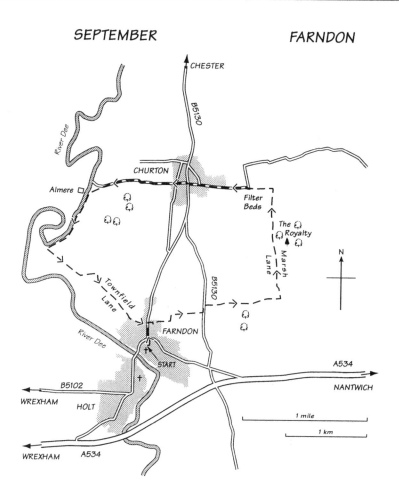

Continue for a considerable distance along Marsh Lane to pass The Royalty, a woodland, on your right and then a brick house after which, for a while, the hedge on your right gives way to wooden fence. Look out for Stone Cottage, also on your right. This small house, a mixture of brick and stone, has a cast-iron notice from the London and North Western Railway fixed to the wall.

Beyond Stone Cottage the lane widens and becomes hedged once again but there is a more open aspect on either side. Soon the lane bends through ninety degrees to the left and acquires a surface as it passes to the left of some filter beds owned by Welsh Water PLC. Beyond these there is a very slight, almost imperceptible climb into Churton, rising from 14 metres above sea level to 26.

On the outskirts of the village Marsh Lane becomes Pump Lane which is lined by attractive houses and cottages with their colourful gardens. Even their hanging baskets still look good. Pass the old-fashioned pump on your right and the impressive timber-framed Churton Hall Farm on your left before reaching the cross-roads formed by the B5130.

Cross to the far pavement, turn right, and after a couple of metres and by the White Horse, turn left into Hob Lane. After 150 metres an intersection is reached. Maintain direction into Knowl Lane which is signed as a footpath. Once more this is hedged; with a grass surface and with the Welsh hills ahead, it provides some excellent, relaxed walking.

After half a kilometre, a three-armed footpath finger post is reached indicating a path to Farndon striking off to the left. Ignore this. Instead, continue along Knowl Lane which is signed to the River Dee. Negotiate a stile alongside a metal five-barred gate and maintain direction along an obvious track that first clings to the hedge on your right which forms the field boundary and then enters a plantation consisting principally of poplars and rowan.

A three-armed footpath post stands at the point where Knowl Lane meets the English bank of the River Dee. The facing house on the Welsh side is Almere.

Turn left along the riverside path signed to Farndon. Almost at once, there is a speed restriction sign for river traffic. Although the path remains close to the Dee the river is generally screened from view by a row of trees. After some distance negotiate a stile and stay forward along the right-hand boundary of an arable field until reaching a wooden five-barred gate by a small, pre-fabricated building. Adjacent is a stile. Beyond this continue in the same direction, staying to the left of a hedge which is all that separates you from the river.

A few metres before the far end of this field the River Dee bends sharply through ninety degrees to the right. At this point, some 10 metres before the facing field boundary, turn right to negotiate a stile and then follow the distinct path for 20 metres until passing through the hedge gap onto Townfield Lane.

Turn left along this. Pass a TV mast on the left and a pig farm on the right but ignore all paths and bridleways going off to the side. Remain along Townfield Lane until it emerges onto Churton Road in Farndon, facing the Primary School. Turn right to retrace your steps to the starting point.

October

Lyme Park

An upland walk which not only provides excellent views of the Peak District and Cheshire Plain but also enables the walker to experience at first hand the rutting behaviour of the red deer.

Route: Lyme Park – Knightslow Wood – Moorside Quarry – Andrew's Knob – Brink Farm – Sponds Hill – Bowstones – Lyme Park.

Terrain: A mixture of moorland paths and tracks, mainly well defined. There are some steep and long climbs.

Start: The car park, Lyme Park, near Disley. Map reference 963824.

Distance: 7½ miles. (12 kilometres)

Map: OS Explorer 268 - Macclesfield & Congleton

Public Transport: The start of the walk is approximately one mile from the entrance to Lyme Park which is served by frequent daily (including Sundays) buses from Manchester, Stockport, Buxton, Bakewell, Matlock and Nottingham. Trains from Buxton and Manchester stop at Disley Station, half a mile from the main entrance. On Saturdays and Sundays a free courtesy bus operates from the main entrance to the car park between 11.00 am and 5.00 pm. On Sundays bus service 361 operates between Stockport and the car park.

By Car: The main entrance to Lyme Park is signed off the A6 approximately 6½ miles south of Stockport and half a mile north of Disley.

Refreshments: The Hall Tea Room opens from 11.00 am to 5.00 pm between 26th March and the 30th October (closed Wednesdays and Thursdays). The Lakeside Coffee Shop is open daily from April to October from 11.00 am to 5.00 pm.

The Month

Although it is the tenth month of our year, October was the eighth in the Roman calendar, hence its name. By now, Autumn is already well established and the weather displays harbingers of the winter months ahead, although often it does provide some glorious sunny days. The days, now, are appreciably shorter.

Many, if not all the summer migrants will have departed our shores, the swallows, swifts and song birds having headed off south to warmer climes. However, the number of autumn immigrants exceeds that of those departing with swans, geese and other wading birds arriving to winter on our coasts and estuaries. Flocks of continental blackbirds and thrushes are to be seen, most noticeably redwings and fieldfares which harvest the rich crop of berries to be discovered on hawthorn, rowan, holly and other trees. Waders such as curlew, lapwing and golden plover, which have bred on the uplands of East Cheshire, will move down to the estuaries for the winter.

Many of the summer flowers will have vanished for another year but bedraggled specimens of rosebay willowherb and foxglove may still be seen amongst the dank grasses and nettles of the hedgerows. Himalayan Balsam will still be weighed down with clusters of seed-heads waiting to explode or be exploded by the fingers of passing walkers.

Despite all these signs October is one of the most colourful months of the year as the leaves of our deciduous trees change colour prior to falling. Woodlands are vibrant with a range of colours from green to yellow and vermilion to gold with other shades in between. As they fall, the dried leaves provide a carpet on the floor which rustles whenever a pair of walking boots pass by.

The stoat begins to assume its coat of winter ermine, the bats go into hibernation and badgers spend more and more time underground. Other animals such as the fox remain active and there is still much more to be seen in the countryside.

Most of all October is the month of the rut. It is the breeding season of the deer. In Lyme Park and other places throughout the county where the red deer is to be found the air is filled with the roaring challenges of the stags as they collect and then defend their harem of females. Younger stags challenge the established males, and as they face up to each other, the air is wrent by the clicking of their antlers. Occasionally some are seriously if not mortally wounded.

October is the month closely associated with the supernatural, the lengthening of the evenings often creating a feeling of fear and of evil spirits amongst country people. It was also popular in many places for divinations, various practices being followed whereby young, single woman would try to discover the identity of their future husbands. It was also a popular month for harvest festivals or fairs, one of the best known in Cheshire being that at Stockport which was held, according to its charter, on St Wilfrid's Day, the 23rd October.

Universally celebrated throughout England is Hallowe'en, the Feast of All Hallows. Much of its religious significance has long since been forgotten but there still lingers a great deal of superstition involving ghosts and spirits.

In Cheshire and several neighbouring counties the direction of the wind on All Hallows would determine the direction for the subsequent three months. Some general weather omens for you to observe include:

"Warm October, cold February."
"As the weather is in October so it will be next March".
"If October bring heavy frosts and wind, then January and February be mild."

Along the way

Lyme Park

In 1398 Richard II made a grant of land in the Royal Forest of Macclesfield to Piers Legh and so the Lyme Estate was created. It remained the home of the family for more than 600 years and when they left, it passed into the ownership of the National Trust. At various times it has been administered by Cheshire County Council and Stockport Metropolitan Borough Council but financial difficulties resulted a few years ago in it being taken back into the sole administration of the National Trust. Recently several developments have taken place including a re-design of some of the gardens, the refurbishment of Lyme Cage and the restoration of the Lime Avenue.

Lyme Hall dates from medieval times but was drastically altered in Tudor times and its present Palladian style is due to Giacomo Leoni in the 1730s. Further additions and alterations were designed by Sir Lewis Wyatt after 1813, when the main features of the garden were created.

The Hall contains collections of historic furniture, tapestries and paintings. There are carvings by Grinling Gibbons and the Sir Francis Legh clock collection. Recently the Grand Staircase and the Bright Gallery have been faithfully restored.

Mary Queen of Scots is known to have enjoyed the hospitality of Lyme Hall when she was a prisoner of Queen Elizabeth 1. At the time she was in the custody of the Earl of Shrewsbury and was staying in nearby Buxton.

Lyme Cage

Lyme Cage is a tall, square stone tower standing on Cage Hill which is on your left as you travel up the drive from the main entrance to the Hall. It was erected in 1524 as a viewing tower for spectators of the hunt. It was later used as a lock-up or prison for poachers and then, until as recently as 1974, served as the residence of the head park keeper. Empty since then, it has been refurbished recently and is open to members of the public on certain days during the summer months.

Lyme Cage

Knightslow Wood

Knightslow Wood derives its name from the legend of Piers Legh who was fatally wounded at the Battle of Agincourt in 1422. According to tradition his body was brought home from France and buried under the mound of Knightslow, Low being the Saxon word for a burial place. Hence, the burial place of a knight. It appears that his daughter Blanche was so upset by his death, that she committed suicide by drowning herself in the River Bollin. Her ghost, the so-called White Lady, still searches for her father's grave.

Lime Avenue

Through a gap in the trees as you walk through Knightslow Wood you will see Lime Avenue. This is believed to have been created during the seventeenth century by Richard Legh and the trees are pruned in such a fashion as to permit a view of the south entrance to the Hall.

The Avenue has only recently been re-opened after being closed for twelve months to allow many of the 150-year-old lime trees, which were dying, to be replaced. The limes are a species unique to Lyme and so the replacements have had to be nurtured from cuttings taken from these trees and grown at the National Trust's own tree nursery.

The Bowstones

The Bowstones remain something of an enigma. Their name would suggest that they were once used for the stringing of bows but, if that were so, why would they be found at such a high altitude? Some experts suggest that they are of Saxon origin, perhaps the bases of either preaching or market crosses. On the other hand they might have been guide posts for travellers crossing over the exposed moorlands. In this respect it is interesting to note that they stand alongside one of the most ancient ridge routes in the Pennines. Another theory holds that they were boundary markers for the Royal Forest of Macclesfield which was much larger during the Middle Ages and of which the Lyme Estate once formed a part.

Two stone shafts, preserved at Lyme Hall, are believed to have formed part of the Bowstones.

Sponds Hill

Sponds Hill is traversed by the Gritstone Trail and its Triangulation Pillar stands at 410 metres above sea level. Close to the bridleway is a viewfinder erected by the Council for the Protection of Rural England in 1975 to mark the European Architectural Year. It highlights landmarks that are visible on a clear day including Winter Hill on the West Pennine Moors to the north, Kinder Scout to the east, the Berwyn Mountains in Wales and the Wrekin in Shropshire.

The Gritstone Trail

The Gritstone Trail is an 18-mile route devised by Cheshire County Council along the East Cheshire uplands. In the north it starts in the car park at Lyme Park and passes Sponds Hill, White Nancy, Teggs Nose, and Croker Hill before reaching Rushton Spencer where it links with the Staffordshire Way.

Route Directions

With your back to the Information Centre walk diagonally left across the car park and the large open area of grass. The small lake is on your right, the children's playground on your left. By a wooden finger post bearing the legend "Gritstone Trail", turn left to negotiate a wooden kissing gate within 10 metres. Follow the wide track as it climbs Drinkwater Meadow, staying close to a stone wall on the left, while enjoying an open aspect over the parkland to your right.

Soon there is a belt of coniferous trees on your left and this shortly develops into a wood. As you climb higher there is a commanding view out towards Stockport and Manchester. After several hundred metres the track curves left to a wooden five-barred gate with an extremely high ladder stile adjacent. Beyond the going levels as the wide track passes through the mixed deciduous trees of Knightslow Wood to another high ladder stile with a footpath post alongside after approximately 500 metres.

Ignore the forward path signed to Bowstones. Instead, turn right along another track which initially remains close to the park's boundary wall. After dipping to cross Poynton Brook, it climbs again before levelling and narrowing into a path as it moves left away from the wall to traverse the lower contours of Park Moor for a considerable distance to a stile. Beyond this the path reverts to another wide track, Moorside Lane.

Ignoring all side paths, proceed along this with first Planted Moor and then Bakestonedale Moor on your left. Pass Moorside Farm on

your right and Moorside Quarry on your left. This only ceased working in 1987. Just beyond, emerge onto the minor road linking Pott
Shrigley with Charles Head and Kettleshulme. Turn left along the
narrow road to walk through the tiny industrial estate on a site formerly occupied by a brickworks.

Stay with the road for a short distance as it twists and turns while
climbing gently to reach a signed bridleway on your left, which
leads up onto Bakestonedale Moor.

Ignore this. Instead continue for a further 100 metres and, by a
footpath signpost, turn right over a stile to ascend steeply for some
200 metres while remaining to the immediate left of a wall. Andrew's Knob is a short distance to your left with a fine prospect of
Bakestonedale Moor beyond that.

As the gradient levels, remain close to the wall on your right, enjoying fine views in all directions which embrace the Cheshire
Plain, White Nancy, the monument high above the village of
Bollington erected to celebrate the victory of Waterloo, Alderley
Edge and the Welsh Mountains. This extensive upland plateau is the
home of hundreds of swallows hawking on the wing and, at all times
of the year, it is not unusual to see a hovering kestrel.

In the first field corner pass through a gap in the facing wall and
maintain direction along the boundary of the subsequent field, still
with a wall on your right, until reaching a five-barred metal gate in
the next field corner. This bears a Gritstone Trail waymark indicating the route for the descent of Gorsey Brow towards Bollington.

Ignore this and do not negotiate the gate. Rather turn sharp left.
The path, not always distinct on the ground, climbs almost imperceptibly alongside the wall on your immediate right from 300 metres
to 350 metres above sea level. In the next field corner the path forms
a T-junction with a wide track which leads to Sherrow Booth Farm, a
short distance to your right. Turn right along this, negotiate a cattle
grid at once and, within a few yards, fork left across the grass for 10
metres to a stile bearing the painted letters, "F.P.".

Follow the path through a scattering of windblown trees, then
pass through a gap in the facing wall. Continue forward though gradually easing towards the derelict wall on your left, aiming for a dead
tree standing in splendid isolation.

OCTOBER   LYME PARK

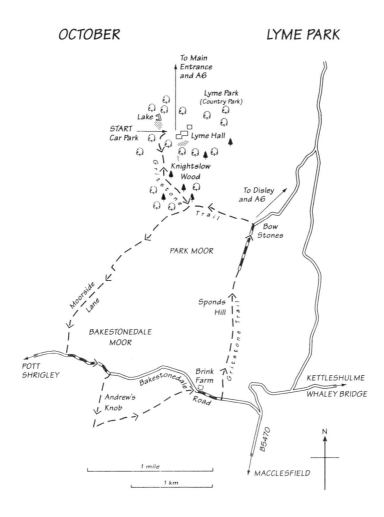

Beyond this tree, follow the broken wall to the left as it rounds Ellis Bank to reach an abandoned quarry below Andrew's Knob. Because of the layered structure of the stone quarried here, it was in great demand for street paving and roofing during the 18th and 19th centuries. There are still a few relics of the quarry buildings.

On meeting a track on a bend, stay forward for about 20 metres to a T-junction. Turn right and pass to the left of a pond as the track climbs slightly before losing a little altitude to a stile adjacent to a five-barred gate by Brink Farm which occupies the summit of the road linking Pott Shrigley to Kettleshulme.

Turn right. Pass the farm and a very low cottage on your right. On reaching a footpath sign turn left over a stile bearing the symbol of the Gritstone Trail, a letter "G" set into the base of a boot.

The bridleway climbs fairly steeply for about 100 metres to a stile alongside another five-barred gate but, beyond this, the gradient eases and very quickly the track reaches the summit of Sponds Hill at a height of 410 metres above sea level.

All climbing is now finished. The wide track runs along the crest of the ridge for more than a mile until reaching Bowstonegate. Pass through a second five-barred gate, turn left over a stile and aim for a very conspicuous ladder stile.

The Bowstones, protected by a fence, are on your right. Over the stile, follow the badly eroded moorland path as it loses altitude until reaching the ladder stile and five-barred gate which permit access to Knightslow Wood. Follow your outward route through the wood and down the parkland to the car park.

November

Alderley Edge

A walk designed to enjoy the full flavour of the autumn colours as it weaves its way through open country and mature woodland which is laced with history and magic. On clear days it rewards all effort with outstanding views.

Route: Car Park–Edge House–Hill Top Farm–Clock House Wood–Glaze Hill – Findlow Farm – Stormy Point – Car Park

Terrain: A mixture of woodland and field paths, including some bridleways. Several small and one very steep climb.

Start: The National Trust car park, by the B5087, Macclesfield Road, Alderley Edge. Map reference 859773.

Distance: 3½ miles (5.3 kilometres).

Map: OS Explorer 268 - Macclesfield & Congleton

Public Transport: Alderley Edge station, 1½ miles from the start, is served by trains from Manchester, Stockport, Wilmslow and Crewe. Alderley Edge village, one mile from the start, is served by frequent daily (including Sundays) buses from Manchester, Wilmslow and Macclesfield.

By Car: Alderley Edge village lies on the A34 between Wilmslow and Congleton. If approaching from the north turn left at the southern end of the village onto the B5087. From here, the car park is approximately one mile. It is signed and has public toilets.

Refreshments: The Wizard Tea Rooms serve light refreshments and drinks between 11.30 am and 5.00 pm on Saturdays and Sundays all year. Bar meals are available at the adjacent Wizard Hotel. There are cafes in the village.

The Month

The name November is derived from the Latin, Novem, meaning the ninth month of the Roman year. In the Christian calendar it commences on the first of the month with the Feast of All Saints followed a day later by All Souls' Day when the souls of the dead are prayed for. In former times, it was regarded as one of the most impor-

tant feasts of the Church. Consequently, various customs developed
including the lighting of bonfires, the ringing of church bells and
'souling'. In Cheshire it was the practice of both children and adults
to go from door to door begging for Soul Cakes and, in return, per-
forming a small play or singing a 'souling song'. In Malpas this read:

> *"Soul! Soul! a soul cake;*
> *Good mistress, gi'us a soul-cake,*
> *One for Pete, one for Paul and one for them as made us all."*

At Northwich and Tarporley the soulers were accompanied by a
hobby-horse and in some Cheshire villages they blackened their
faces. At Bosley, south of Macclesfield, the plays performed had
traces of the medieval Miracle Plays or were centred around St
George and the Dragon.

In a wider sense a soul-cake was any present such as an apple,
money or a bowl of beer given to the souling party at the door; in the
strictest sense, it was a cake or a small loaf similar to Madeira Cake
but spiced. Milk and eggs were the principal ingredients.

In more recent times, these two feasts have been overshadowed
by Bonfire Night which began with the suppression of the Gunpow-
der Plot of 1605 and is celebrated by the universal lighting of bonfires and the burning of effigies of Guy Fawkes.

Another important Church festival was the Feast of St Martin, or
Martinmas, on the 11th November which was an important day in
the agrarian calendar for the payment of rents and dues. Not surprisingly it was another day celebrated with drinking and revelry as
commemorated in the song:

> *"It is the day of Martinmasse.*
> *Cuppes of ale should freelie pass:*
> *What though the Wynter has begunne,*
> *To push down the summer sunne,*
> *To our fire we can betake.*
> *And enjoy the crackling brake*
> *Never heeding Wynter's face."*

In the days when England was primarily an agrarian country and
there was no Meteorological Office with hourly forecasts on radio
and television the weather lore associated with many of these feast

days often assumed crucial importance. One very important day was the Feast of St Martin:

> "If the wind is south-westerly at Martinmas it keeps it there till after Christmas."

or

> "When the ice before Martinmas bears a duck then look for a winter of mire and muck".

However, sometimes fair, mild weather was often the general experience about this period and so gave rise to the expression, "St Martin's little summer".

In November the weather may be variable but, in fairness, this makes it little different from any other month of the year, such is the fickleness of the British climate. In general, however, it is often a month of fog, rain, dark clouds and a general feeling that winter has started. The days are shorter and the atmosphere gloomy. The glorious colours of October have largely disappeared and, apart from some oak leaves which stubbornly still cling to the branches, the de-

The view across the Cheshire Plain from the Edge

ciduous trees are mainly leafless, the branches often dripping water collected either from rain or the damp, murky atmosphere.

It is not unusual for the hills and moorlands of East Cheshire to experience their first snow of the winter and frosts may be severe. Along the Dee Estuary the migrant birds from Europe and elsewhere swell the population of wading birds and in the county as a whole there is an influx of fieldfares, redwings, thrushes, blackbirds, serin and siskin. In parts of Cheshire it is not unusual to see flocks of long-tailed tits combing the hedgerows in search of small insects or, sometimes, seed heads.

Many mammals begin their winter hibernation, particularly bats and badgers, while in the uplands the mountain hare begins to change its blue-grey summer pelage for its white winter coat, as does the stoat. The natural world may appear to slow down but for the observant walker there is still plenty of activity to notice.

Along the way

Alderley Edge

Alderley Edge is one of several sandstone escarpments rising from the Cheshire Plain, the others being the Peckforton Hills, Helsby Hill and Frodsham Hill. Now well wooded, its summits command extensive views embracing Kinder Scout, Bleaklow and the North Pennine Moors.

Formed more than 200 million years ago, it rises steeply to over 600 feet above sea level. Until trees were planted by Sir Thomas Stanley in the sixteenth century and his descendants 200 years later, the slopes were either bare or covered with grass. Even in pre-historic times the Edge was exploited by humans in search of iron, copper and lead, and this tradition of mining was continued by the Romans. Much of this industrial activity was centred around Stormy Point where one relic is the bare earth.

The largest of several mines exploited was the Engine Vein and during the eighteenth century the industry flourished. One mine employed no fewer than 50 men and made a profit of £2,500 a year. Mining continued on Alderley Edge until the close of the First World War but several mine shafts remain. It is possible to visit these under the supervision of the local caving club, The Derbyshire Caving Club. In total, there are more than 12 miles of passageways under the Edge and an excavation by archaeologists from Manchester University in 1998 revealed new evidence of mining during the Bronze Age.

Beacon Point is another landmark. It was here that in 1588, before the first trees were planted, that a bonfire was lit to signal the approach of the Spanish Armada, one of a series which stretched from Cornwall to the Scottish Borders – a primitive but affective Early Warning System. Until it was destroyed by a storm in 1931 there was a small hut nearby where the pitch and other materials were stored in case it was required again. Today there is a commemorative plaque.

On Castle Rock the traces of the foundations of a castle have been unearthed but it is thought that the project was abandoned in favour of the site now occupied by Beeston Castle, much closer to the Welsh border.

The most famous event in Alderley's history is based on legend which tells of a farmer crossing the Edge with a horse which he wished to sell. He was approached by Merlin, the Wizard, who tapped the rock with his staff and a pair of iron gates appeared. They opened with a tremendous noise and Merlin encouraged the old man to enter. In a huge cavern he saw a hoard of treasure and a group of soldiers were sleeping. Their leader was King Arthur and Merlin informed the farmer that he was sleeping there until the day that England needed him again. When that time came he would emerge, win a great battle and save the country. It is this incident which gives the local public house its name. It is a name which has also been given to the Wizard's Well which is formed by a natural spring and which is now exploited by a mineral water company.

The Village, which takes its name from the Edge, was formerly the home of one of the branches of the Stanley family. One member achieved some fame as the Dean of Westminster. With the advent of the railway in the nineteenth century Alderley developed as a commuter village patronised by the wealthy cotton magnates and business men of Manchester, many of whom built fine houses on the lower slopes above the village. In fact, the railway company rewarded such men with a silver medal, to be worn on their watch chains, which entitled them to free first class travel to and from Manchester.

Route Directions

Exit the car park by the western end, taking the path which passes between two low hawthorn hedges. After approximately 30 metres, and facing the Wizard Tea Rooms and the National Trust Information Centre, turn right along the broad track or bridleway which goes in a north-easterly direction, passing Forester's Lodge on your left and with distant views of Shutlingsloe to your right.

Half-way through the first bend veer right along a very short path to an unsigned gap to the left of a wooden five-barred gate. Note that the rear of one of the posts is waymarked.

Follow the path, lined with intermittent clumps of ragwort and gorse, as it traverses a field between two wire fences, dipping slightly and then rising to meet a wide track. Cross this directly and, with a red brick house on your immediate left, continue along another wide grassy track as its loses height gradually to a waymarked stile adjacent to a broken, wooden five-barred gate.

Stay forward, passing a large dead tree and descending to a stile in the far corner of the field. Turn right over this and advance to the right of a wire fence for 50 metres before making a left turn, this time over a stile by a metal five-barred gate. This provides access to another wide track with a combined hawthorn and bramble hedge on the left and a wire fence on the right. It leads to a wooden, waymarked stile positioned between two metal five-barred gates. Stay forward between two wire fences to another stile, also waymarked.

Over this chose the left-hand path which clings to the hedge on your left. Hill Top Farm is a short distance to your right. Follow this boundary around the edge of the field, passing two small ponds in the first corner until reaching another waymarked stile in the subsequent corner.

Over this advance a further 10 metres to a waymarker post. Turn left. Ignore another path signed to the right, opting instead to continue directly ahead along a broad path. Soon there is a large wooden

NOVEMBER   ALDERLEY EDGE

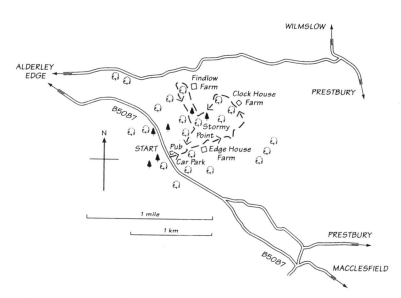

sign shaped to resemble a gravestone which carries the legend, "The Edge".

The track loses altitude as it enters the woods which, at this point consist principally of oak and holly until an opening on the right allows a view of Clock House Farm This is followed by a gentle climb before losing altitude again as you re-enter the woodland.

After a further short distance the path corkscrews down a steep slope before crossing a very narrow stream and swinging left to follow the contour along the very base of the Edge and just inside the perimeter fence of the woods. The path passes one of the famous mines, Hough Level, which has a short stretch of railway track emerging from its entrance.

Continue along the low-level path, enjoying distant views of Werneth Low and Kinder Scout, until gaining a large, open area just before Findlow Farm which is on your right. There is no sign or waymark at this point but take the clear, distinct path on the left which climbs the steep flank of Alderley Edge for a considerable distance before emerging onto a saddle or ridge. Ignore the forward continuation of the path, instead turn left along another path which climbs diagonally through a very shallow gully to emerge finally on the crest of the Edge, a few metres to the right of Stormy Point.

This landmark is recognisable by the large expanses of exposed rock and old mine workings not to mention the expansive views which embrace not only Kinder Scout and Bleaklow, but Winter Hill and Great Hill on the West Pennine Moors to the north of Bolton. Closer at hand it is easy to distinguish Lyme Cage and Bowstonegate in Lyme Park.

Stormy Point is also recognisable by the memorial plaque in memory of Lawrence and Mary Gavin Pilkington who also enjoyed these views. Their daughters gave the Edge to the National Trust in 1949 with some financial assistance from Cheshire County Council.

Walk round Stormy Point, ignoring three paths leading off to the right and continuing round until meeting a broad track running to the immediate right of a wire fence. Turn right along this and follow it until passing through a narrow gap alongside a wooden barrier. Turn right onto a bridleway, which soon passes another old mining area on the right. One hundred metres beyond this mine, the track re-joins the outward route which should be followed back to the car park.

December

Delamere Forest

An ideal route for a cold winter's day, this level but mainly woodland walk passes through a wonderland of Christmas trees in preparation for the big day.

Route: Delamere Forest Visitor Centre—Linmere Moss—Eddisbury Lodge—Black Lake — Battleaxe Road — Switchback Road — Barnsbridge Gates — Sandstone Trail — -Spiv Road — Linmere Cottages — -Visitor Centre.

Start: Visitor Centre, Delamere Forest. Map reference 551705.

Distance: 6½ miles (10.3 kilometres).

Maps: OS Explorer 267 - Northwich & Delamere Forest.

Public Transport: There are several trains daily, including Sundays, from Stockport, Manchester and Chester which stop at Delamere station, approximately half a mile from the Visitor Centre. There are no bus services.

By Car: Delamere Forest and the Visitor Centre are signed from the A556 at the Vale Abbey Arms. If travelling from the Manchester direction turn right onto the B5152 signed to Frodsham. Delamere station is reached after one mile. If travelling from the Chester direction turn left onto the B5152.

Visitor Centre: Open every day except Christmas Day, 10.30 am to 4.30 pm. Phone: 01606 882167.

Refreshments: Drinks and confectionery are available at the Visitor Centre. The Station House Cafe at Delamere station provides a full range of meals and drinks throughout the day. Open 10.00 am to 5.00 pm daily, including Sundays, all year.

The Month

December takes its name from *Decem*, the tenth month of the Roman year but for us it is the twelfth or last. By now, winter is confirming its grip, often with low temperatures and sometimes even with snow. The days are at their shortest but, despite the murk and the gloom, there are usually some bright days in which to enjoy a good brisk walk.

The first part of the month is Advent. It is celebrated by a wreath bearing four candles, one being lit on each of the four Sundays preceding Christmas Day. However, it is Christmas, with Boxing day following, which dominates the month and the weeks beforehand tend to disappear in a round of school concerts, Nativity Plays and seasonal shopping, leaving little time for long distance walking. Nowadays the seasonal holiday for most people extends from Christmas Eve into the New Year so, after the immediate festivities of December 25th, there is ample time for getting out and about. After the vast amounts of food eaten, a long walk is probably essential.

This is not the place to delve into all the well-known Christmas customs but, for the outdoor man and woman it is worth remembering that folklore informs us that:

> *"Hours of sun on Christmas day*
> *So many frosts in May".*

or

> *"A green Christmas, a white Easter."*

or

> *"If Christmas on a Sunday be*
> *A windy winter we shall see".*

It is also worth noting that on New Year's Eve

> *"If the wind is in the east*
> *The coming year will be good for fruit:*
> *But if it is in the north-east*
> *Flee it both man and brute."*

In December the countryside appears to be at its most drab and yet it can produce scenes of great beauty. The deciduous trees are bare and skeletal, but to see them adorned with frost is one of the miracles of nature. Often the fields, too, are white with frost and it is not unusual to see ponds, lakes and even canals frozen solid.

Many of the mammals are in hibernation and, unless the weather is exceptionally warm there is little to be seen in the way of insects. In Cheshire, however, especially in the great parks of Lyme, Tatton and Dunham Massey, the herds of deer are to be seen roaming round and grazing. It is still possible to spot stoats and weasels, not to mention the grey squirrels that are so widespread.

Wherever there is a lake or mere, mallard, Canada Geese, moorhen, coot and other water fowl are still active to prove that the countryside is far from completely dormant. On the Dee Estuary the wading birds feed on the foreshore and rise in flocks with the advancing tide.

Most flowers have died for another year, only their dank vegetation remaining but, as you walk through the forests your feet will crunch on the newly fallen leaves. The berries of holly, rowan and hawthorn provide a welcome display of colour as well as food for flocks of thrushes and blackbirds.

The bareness of the landscape also opens-up views which are not available during the lusher summer months and those crystal clear days often provide superior views of the panoramas than do the warm, hazy days of summer.

And, finally, after a good walk on a cold frosty day, there is always the satisfaction of calling in at that cafe for a bowl of piping hot soup or a cup of tea.

Along the way

Delamere Forest

Delamere Forest is the largest area of woodland in Cheshire, covering in excess of 1,300 acres. The name is derived from the French, "de la mere" meaning "of the mere", a reference to the numerous meres and mosses included within its boundary. These resulted from the massive ice sheet which once covered the whole countryside of the county.

Ten thousand years ago the retreating glaciers left enormous blocks of ice behind which gradually melted to create deep hollows which, over the intervening centuries, developed into the area's famous wetlands.

Delamere today is all that remains of the great Norman hunting forests of Mara and Mondrum which stretched from the Mersey in the north to Nantwich in the south. At the heart of the forest lies the deep hollow of Blakemere Moss, an ancient wetland drained by

A track through the bare December trees of Delamere Forest

French Prisoners-Of-War during the Napoleonic Wars. Trees have been grown there ever since.

It remained as a royal hunting ground until the reign of Charles 1 in the seventeenth century. During his years on the throne all the remaining deer were culled and, in later years, the great oaks were used for the building of warships. In the mid-nineteenth century the area was replanted but the seed proved to be of poor quality and little growth took place.

After the First World War the area was taken over by the Forestry Commission and coniferous species were planted to maximise timber production. These included Scots and Corsican Pines, Larch and Western Hemlock. In more recent years, in accordance with changing policy, the forest has been developed as a recreational facility which has resulted in the planting of more broad-leaved species, the provision of car parks, picnic areas, a Visitor Centre and forest trails.

The forest provides a habitat for numerous birds including the greater spotted woodpecker, the green woodpecker, nuthatches, tree creepers and various species of titmice. In winter crossbills and siskins prise the seeds from the pine cones. In summer dragonflies and damsel flies are widespread around the numerous marshy pools and the floor is carpeted with bluebells in Spring. The area is also well blessed with small mammals which attract the attention of the tawny owls and other raptors while the grey squirrel is almost everywhere. The flora includes several species of ferns including the shield fern and bracken.

Eddisbury Hill

By the Old Pale Farm close by the summit of Eddisbury Hill were the ramparts of a Celtic fortress. In AD 915, Ethelfleda, Queen of the Kingdom of Mercia, built a stronghold there against the invading Danes and centuries later a hunting lodge was constructed. This became known as The Chamber in the Forest and was the administrative and judicial centre for the area.

Oakmere

Oakmere was once the largest mere in the forest and legend tells of Mary Ann Hollingworth, "The Old Woman of Oakmere". Around 1815, she lived there in a cottage allegedly made from the ribs of a whale. Various stories circulated about her but the truth was that she was English, had married a German and gone to live in Hanover. After the death of her husband she returned home where she waited to be joined by her son.

One day, while out on the road looking for him, she saw a group of men dump a sack into the lake. Fearing that it was her son, she alerted the authorities who investigated to discover that the sack did indeed contain the body of a man. However, it was not her son because he duly arrived on the following day. The outcome of this story does not appear to have been recorded.

Route Directions

Leave the car park by turning right along the narrow road, passing the cream-coloured Conservancy Offices on your right and the Nursery on your left. After some 200 metres, and by waymarker post number 13, veer right onto a forest track. Linmere Moss is to the

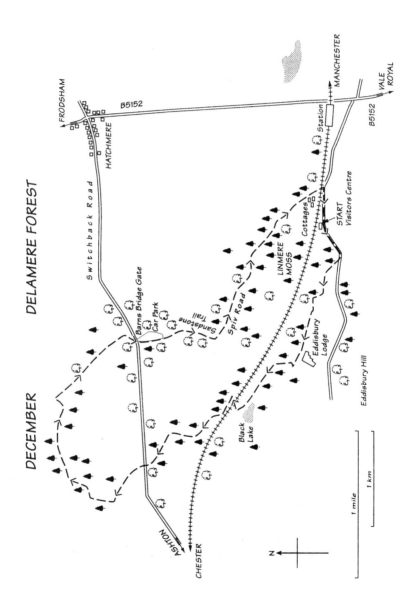

right. The track is enclosed by trees initially but soon there is a fence with open country beyond on the left.

By post number 12 bear right, with the track, as it descends into a shallow valley and climbs briefly before curving left to post number 11. By this, make a left turn, passing through forest once again where considerable recent felling has taken place, at least judging by the large expanse of cleared area. At the next junction, which has no post, turn left with the main track to go downhill and climbing until Eddisbury Lodge is close-by on your left, although barely visible through the trees.

A short distance beyond the track forms a T-junction with the Sandstone Trail, a medium distance trail which runs from Frodsham in the north of the county to Grindley Brook on the Shropshire border. Make a right turn onto another wide track but, by the next Sandstone Trail waymarker post there are three paths radiating off to the left. Take the third one which goes a shade to the right of a clump of pine trees with a spread of birch and bracken on the right. This path is much narrower but its sandy base makes for excellent walking.

Soon Black Lake, a very large expanse of water, is visible through the trees and 100 metres beyond the path meets Battleaxe Road, a somewhat broader track. Turn right to cross over the Manchester to Chester railway line by a sandstone bridge. At the far end of this, by marker post number 43, turn left onto a wide track flanked by more oak and birch. After 250 metres the track forms a T-junction with Spiv Road, yet another broad forest track. Turn left.

At the next junction, number 51, turn right and after 250 metres and by marker post number 44, make a left turn, soon passing a picnic area on your right. Pass to the right of a wooden barrier to meet Switchback Road, so-called because of its undulating nature. Exercising caution because of the speed of passing cars, cross directly onto another track. Ignore the first narrower path to the right after approximately 150 metres but take the second which follows after a further 40 metres. At this point there is no sign of a waymark.

This new, narrow path is peaty, soft and gentle on the feet and, being easy to follow, permits a decent speed. It is flanked with birch, oak, bracken and, behind these, row after row of conifers.

Eventually, after turning and twisting its way through the confines of the forest, it meets a wide track by post number 46. Make a right turn to pass a very large area of birch scrub on your left. The track again twists and turns to another T-junction recognised by post 52. Turn left to pass another large expanse of birch scrub, although this time on your right, with rabbits scurrying from one side of the track to the other.

At the next T-junction, waymarker post number 47, turn right and, at the subsequent T-junction recognised by post number 48, turn right along the Sandstone Trail for the short distance to Barnsbridge Gates. Pass to the side of the wooden anti-vehicle barrier and cross Switchback Road directly to the facing finger post with its attendant Sandstone Trail information panel. Maintain direction southwards through the car park. However, before the far end, take one of the short flight of steps on your right to gain the Sandstone Trail and, at the top, turn left.

At this point the Trail passes through an avenue of large trees, including horse chestnut and oak, with a large lake gradually silting-up on the left. At the first Y-junction, ignore the wheelchair path striking off to the left, rather remaining along the Sandstone Trail which bears slightly to the right.

At post number 18 continue in the same direction before shortly reaching a major intersection of routes with waymarker post number 49. There are also two very large signs, almost like Totem poles, giving directions to cyclists following the White Moor Trail and the Hunger Hill Trail through Delamere. At this intersection leave the Sandstone Trail by making a left turn onto a wide forest track known as Spiv Road. By post number 10 there is a clear view to the right which permits a glimpse of the radio communications tower on Pale Heights and of the adjacent Eddisbury Hill.

Remain forward, ignoring all further side paths and tracks until reaching Linmere Cottages. Immediately beyond waymarker post number 2, re-cross the railway by a stone bridge and turn right along the narrow road leading back to the car park.

Also of Interest:

TOWNS & VILLAGES OF BRITAIN : CHESHIRE
Ron Scholes
From the dawning of Neolithic man to the growth of black and white timbered market towns, Ron Scholes's knowledge of Cheshire's towns, villages, and folklore springs from his deep understanding of the county's landscape. Local historians and visitors will enjoy this informative, readable account.
ISBN 1 85058 637 3 Price £8.95

EAST CHESHIRE WALKS
Graham Beech
The definitive guide to walking in East Cheshire is now in its third edition - and is still outselling all other local walking guides! Completely updated and revised, Graham Beech (partner in Sigma Press with his wife Diana) has also added some new walks, including a 20-mile challenge route which offers magnificent views and real sense of achievement. With 39 walks covering 250 miles, there really is something for everyone!
ISBN 1 85058 593 8 Price £6.95

WEST CHESHIRE WALKS
Jen Darling
This, the companion guide to our East Cheshire book, contains 40 walks reflecting the great variety of landscape between Warrington and Whitchurch to the North and South and from Wilmslow and Wirral to the West and East.
ISBN 1 85058 111 8 Price £6.95

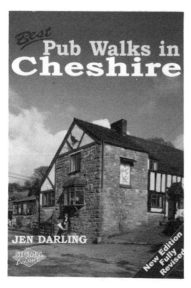

BEST PUB WALKS IN CHESHIRE
Jen Darling

This is the second edition of this well-established book which covers the entire county. Thoroughly updated, it is the most authoritative guidebook to the walks and pubs of Cheshire. Much, however, is unaltered - the same brilliant range of walks and the sparkling detailed descriptions of Cheshire's landscape and rural traditions.

"I was delighted to be asked to put a few words on paper for this new book on 'Pub Walks in Cheshire'. This book brings together a series of suggestions for your enjoyment well worth some of your time." - John Ellis from Cheshire Tourism

ISBN 1 85058 755 8 Price £7.95

BEST TEA SHOP WALKS IN CHESHIRE
Clive Price

Cheshire is the epitome of tea shop country - "...a winning blend of scenic strolls and tasty tea shops" CHESHIRE LIFE.

ISBN 1 85058 455 9 Price £6.95

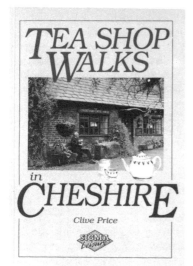

CHESHIRE WALKS WITH CHILDREN
Nick Lambert

This was the first in our "walks with children" series and has quickly become a firm favourite. Things to look out for and questions to answer along the way make it an entertaining book for young and old alike.

ISBN 1 85058 560 1 Price £7.95

All of our books are available through booksellers. In case of difficulty, or for a free catalogue, please contact: **SIGMA LEISURE, 1 SOUTH OAK LANE, WILMSLOW, CHESHIRE SK9 6AR.**
Phone: 01625-531035 Fax: 01625-536800.
E-mail: info@sigmapress.co.uk   Web site: http//www.sigmapress.co.uk
MASTERCARD and VISA orders welcome.